AUTHENTIC TRANSCRIPTIONS
WITH NOTES AND TABLATURE

BIG BILL BROONZY
GUITAR COLLECTION

Cover photo by Gerrit Schilp/Redferns

Music transcriptions by Adonai Booth

ISBN 978-1-5400-4011-4

Visit Hal Leonard Online at
www.halleonard.com

Contact us:
Hal Leonard
7777 West Bluemound Road
Milwaukee, WI 53213
Email: info@halleonard.com

In Europe, contact:
Hal Leonard Europe Limited
42 Wigmore Street
Marylebone, London, W1U 2RN
Email: info@halleonardeurope.com

In Australia, contact:
Hal Leonard Australia Pty. Ltd.
4 Lentara Court
Cheltenham, Victoria, 3192 Australia
Email: info@halleonard.com.au

Baby Please Don't Go

Words and Music by William Lee Conley Broonzy

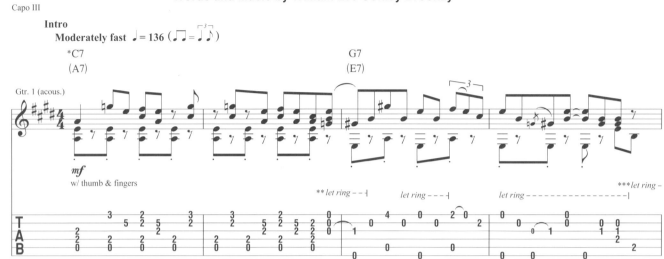

*Symbols in parentheses represent chord names respective to capoed guitar.
Symbols above reflect actual sounding chords. Capoed fret is "0" in tab.

***Pertains to all strings.

**Pertains to strings 1-3 only throughout, except where indicated.

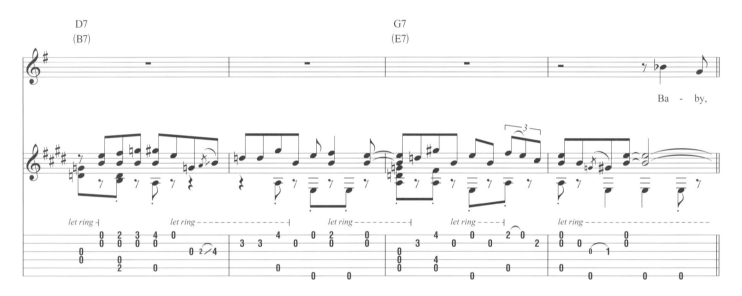

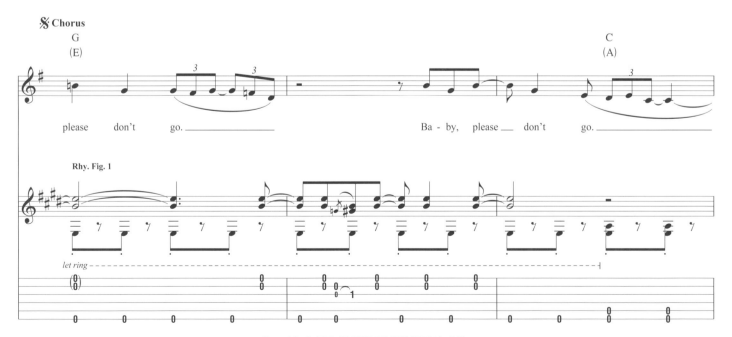

G
(E)

Ba - by, please _____ don't go back to New Or - leans. You know it hurts _____

let ring -

G6
(E6)

G
(E)

_____ me so. _____

1., 2. Babe, I'm _____

End Rhy. Fig. 1

let ring - - - - - - - - - - - - - - - -

let ring -

Verse

Gtr. 1: w/ Rhy. Fig. 1, (1st 6 meas., simile)

G
(E)

C
(A)

way   down   here. _____

You know, I'm   way   down   here. _____

To Coda ⊕

G
(E)

_____ Babe, I'm way _____ down   here _____
{ in a roll - in'   fog. _____ }
{ on old Parch - man's   Farm, _____ } Ba - by, please _____

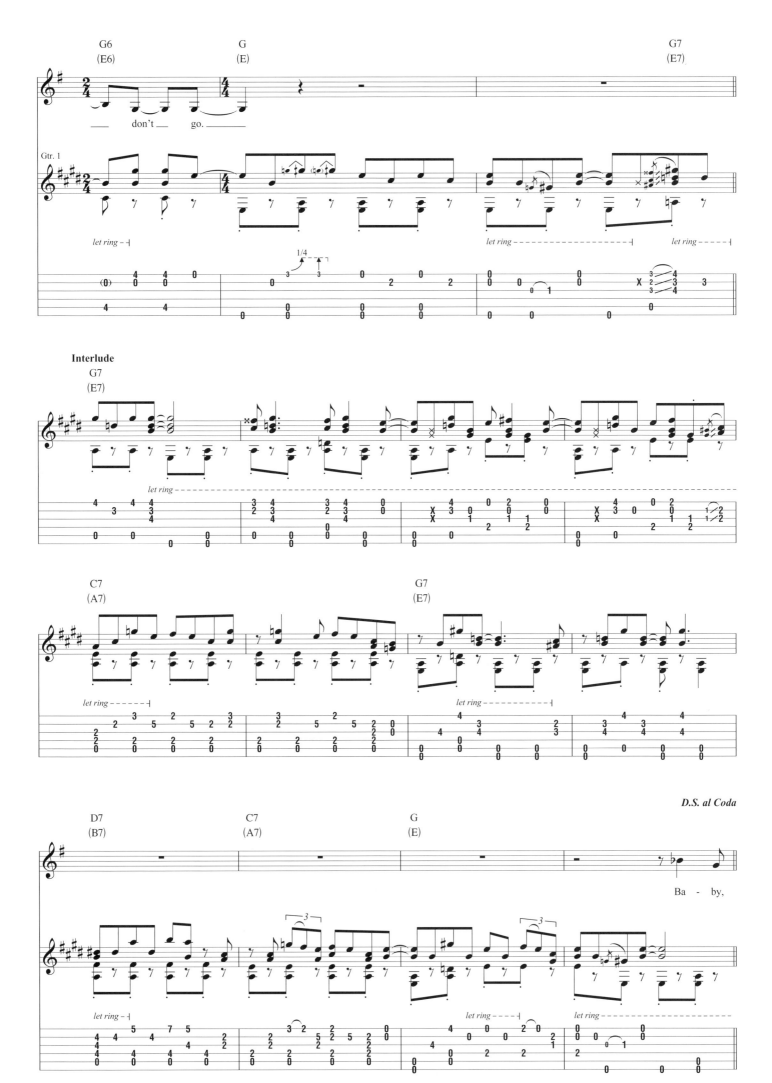

Interlude

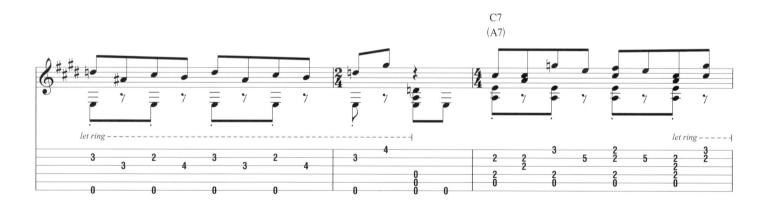

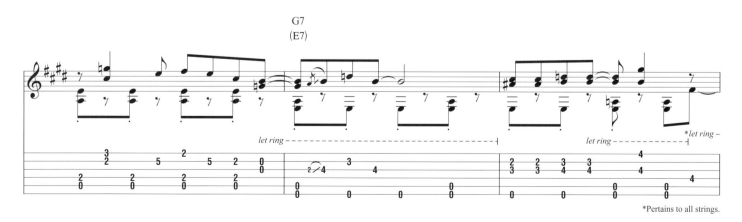

*Pertains to all strings.

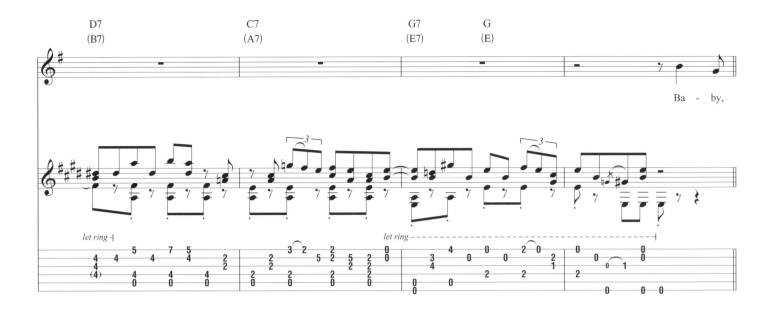

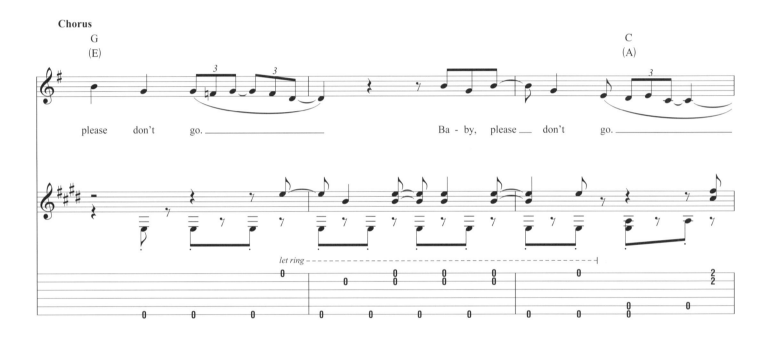

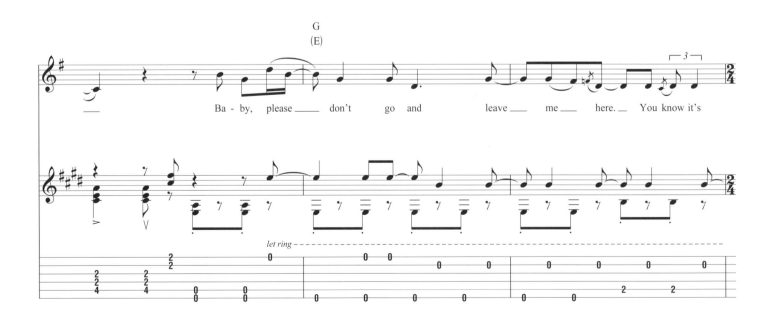

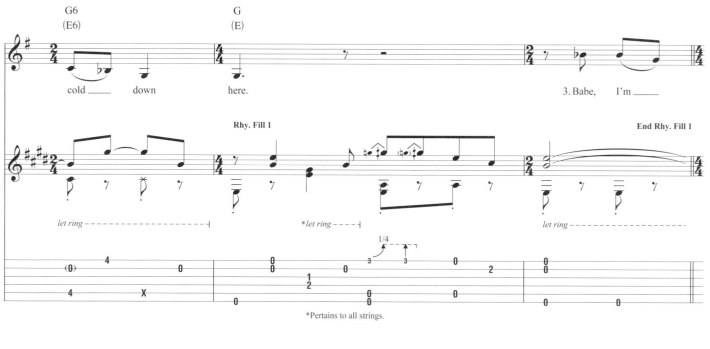

*Pertains to all strings.

Verse

Gtr. 1: w/ Rhy. Fig. 1, simile

way down here. _____ You know, I'm way down here. _____

_____ Babe, I'm way _____ down here on old Parch - man's Farm. ____ Ba - by,

please don't go. _____ 4. You know it's

Verse

Gtr. 1: w/ Rhy. Fig. 1 (1st 7 meas., simile)

cold down here. _____ Babe, it's cold ____ down here. _____

_____ Babe, it's cold _____ down here ____ on old Parch - man's Farm. ____ Ba - by,

*Pertains to all strings.

from *One Beer, One Blues*

Get Back

Words and Music by William Lee Conley Broonzy

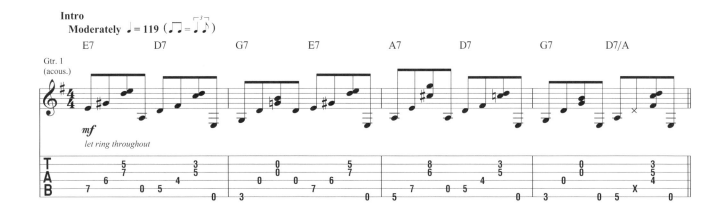

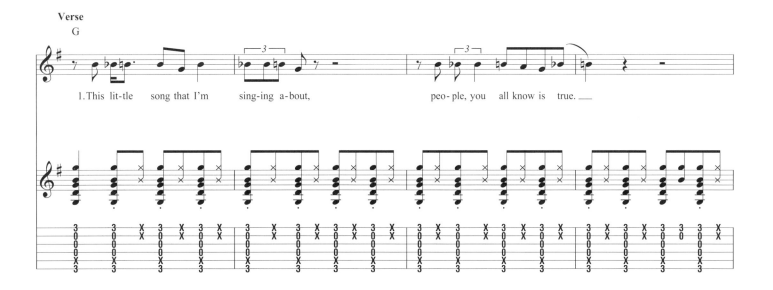

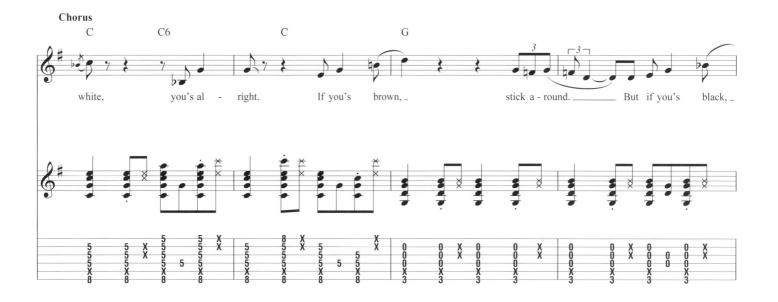

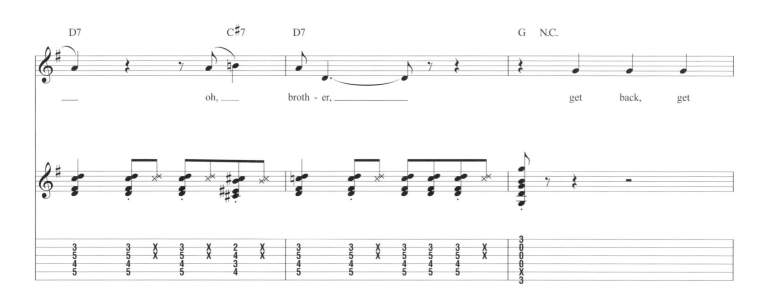

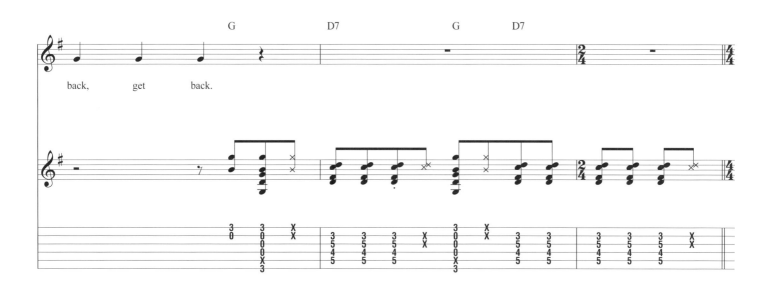

Verse

2. I was in a place ___ one ___ night, they was all ___ hav-ing fun. ___

They was all ___ buy-ing beer and wine, ___ but they would not sell ___ me none. They said if you's

𝄋 Chorus

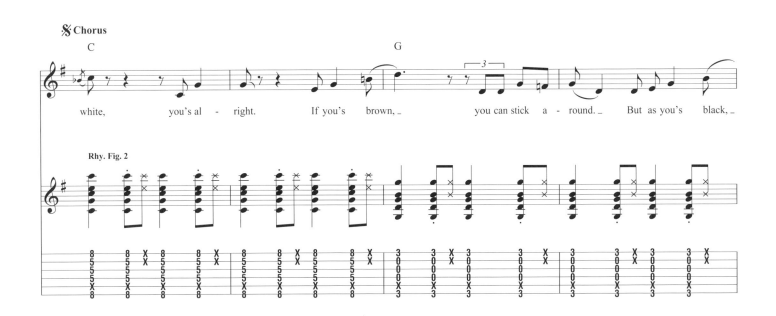

white, you's al - right. If you's brown, ___ you can stick a - round. ___ But as you's black, ___

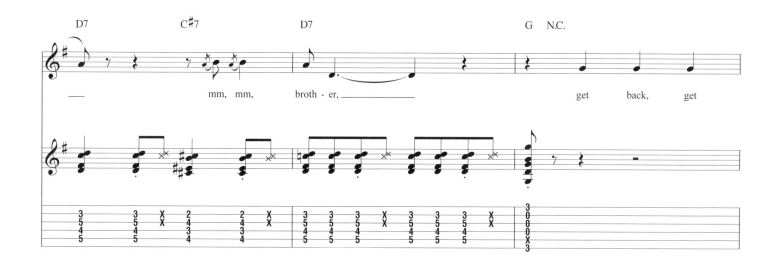

Verse

Gtr. 1: w/ Rhy. Fig. 1

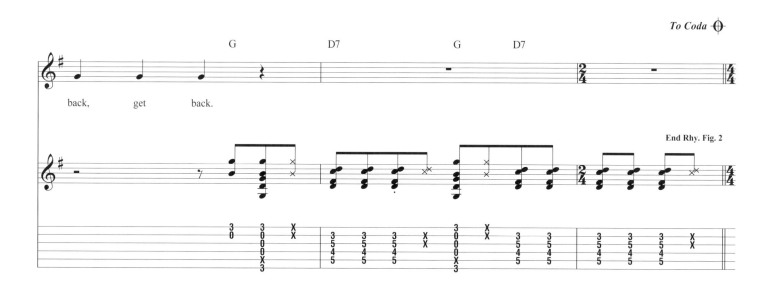

3. I ___ went to an em - ploy - ment of - fice. I got a num-ber and I got in line. ___

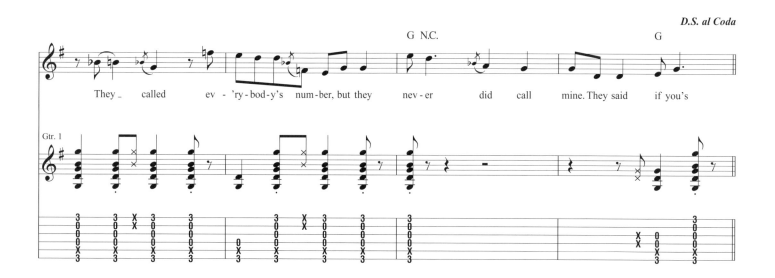

They ___ called ev - 'ry-bod-y's num-ber, but they nev - er did call mine. They said if you's

The Glory of Love

Words and Music by Billy Hill

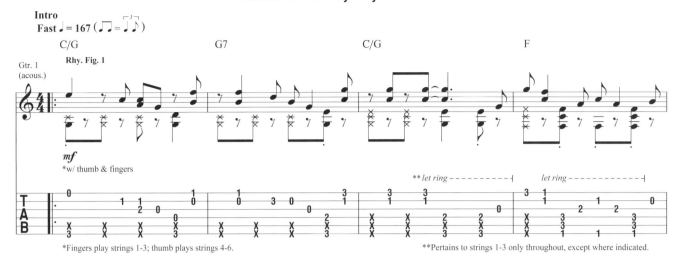

*Fingers play strings 1-3; thumb plays strings 4-6.

**Pertains to strings 1-3 only throughout, except where indicated.

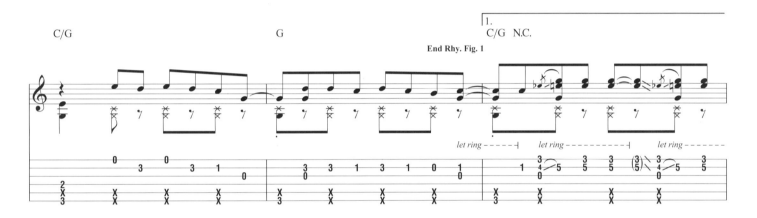

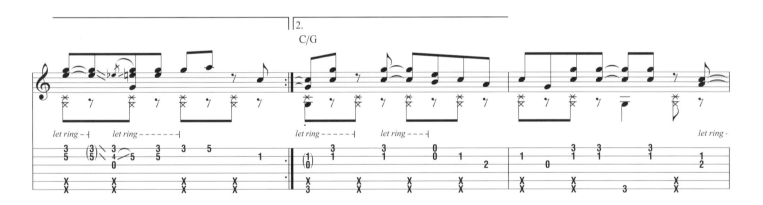

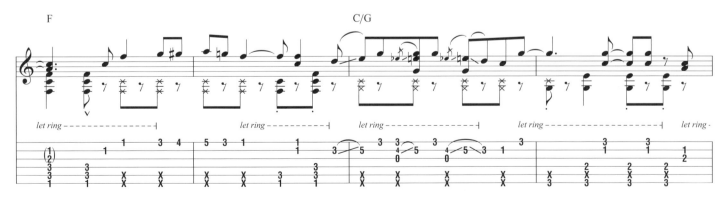

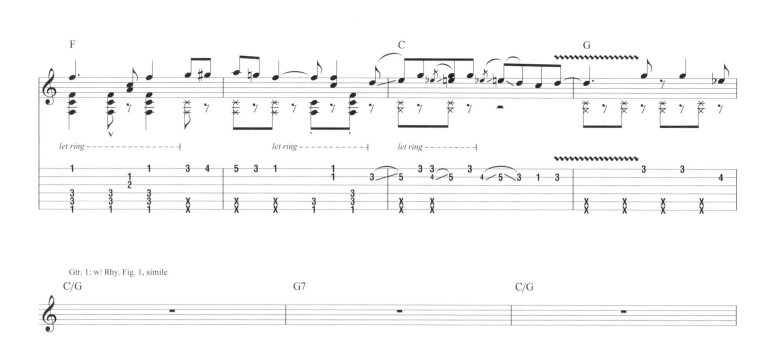

Gtr. 1: w/ Rhy. Fig. 1, simile

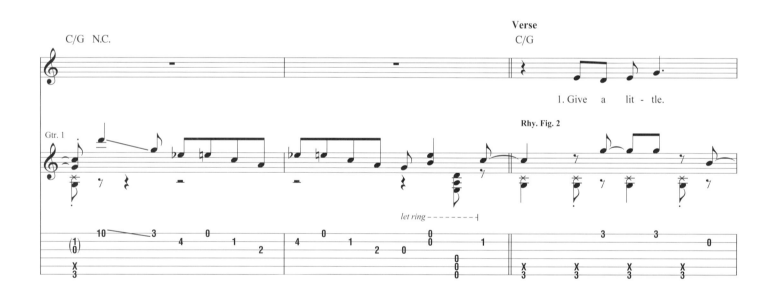

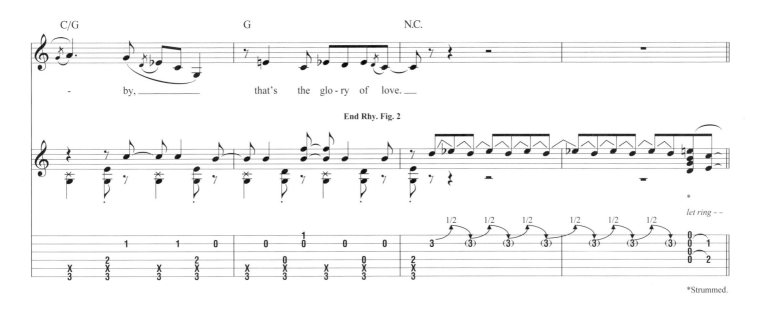

that's the glo-ry of love.

End Rhy. Fig. 2

let ring – –

*Strummed.

Verse

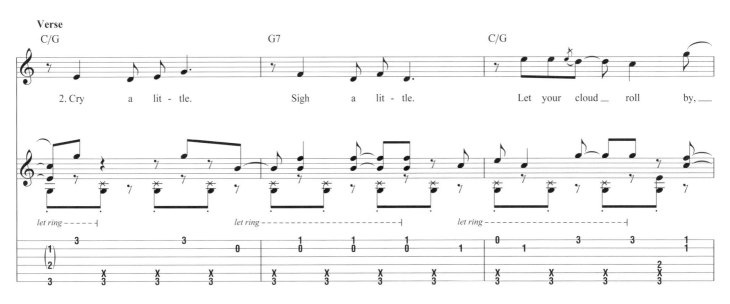

2. Cry a lit-tle. Sigh a lit-tle. Let your cloud roll by,

let ring *let ring* *let ring*

Gtr. 1: w/ Rhy. Fig. 2 (last 3 meas.)

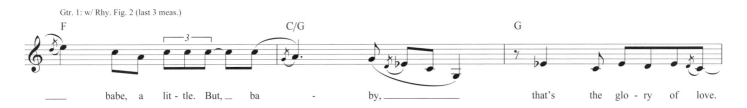

babe, a lit-tle. But, ba - by, that's the glo-ry of love.

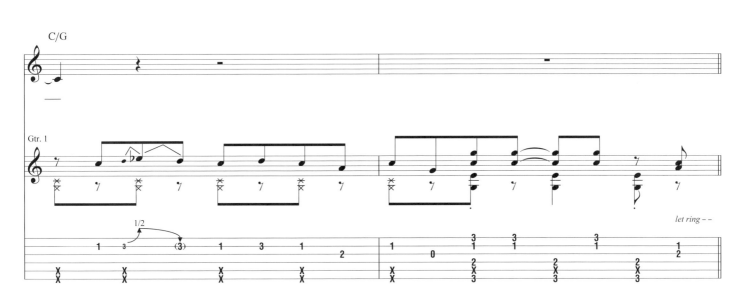

Gtr. 1

let ring – –

Bridge

Long as there are just the two of us, have the world and its charm.

Long as there are just the two of us, hold each oth - er's arm. 3. Ba - by, now,

Verse

Gtr. 1: w/ Rhy. Fig. 2, simile

win just a lit - tle, lose a lit - tle. Some - time have the

blues, babe, a lit - tle. But, ba - by, that's the glo - ry of love.

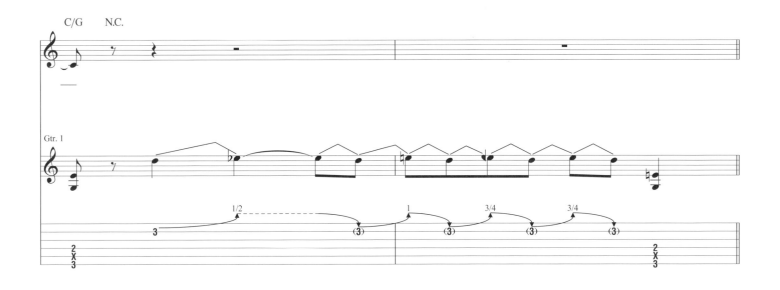

Interlude

Gtr. 1: w/ Rhy. Fig. 1, simile

Gtr. 1: w/ Rhy. Fig. 1, simile

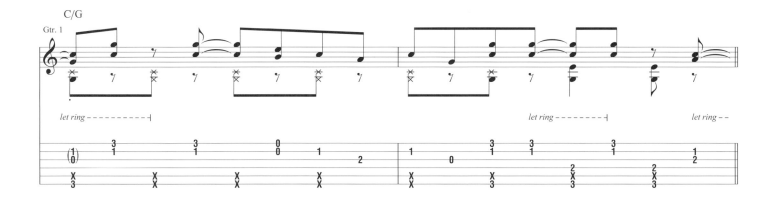

Bridge

Gtr. 1: w/ Rhy. Fig. 3, simile

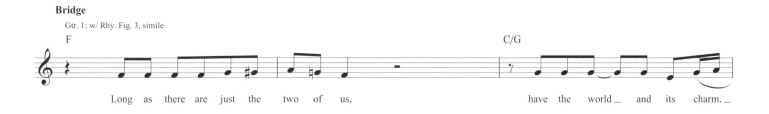

Long as there are just the two of us, have the world and its charm.

Long as there are just the two of us,

Verse

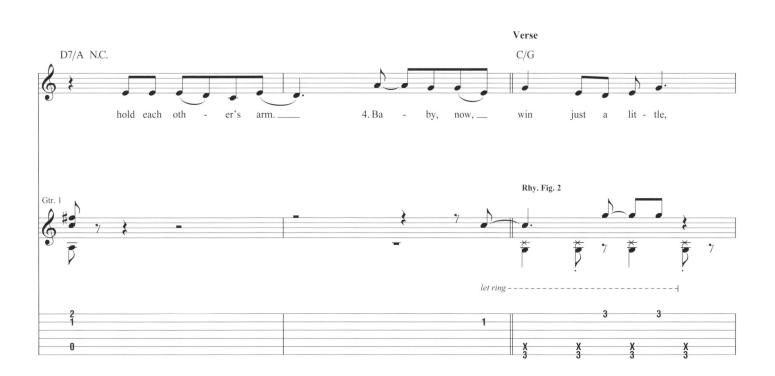

hold each oth-er's arm. 4. Ba - by, now, win just a lit - tle,

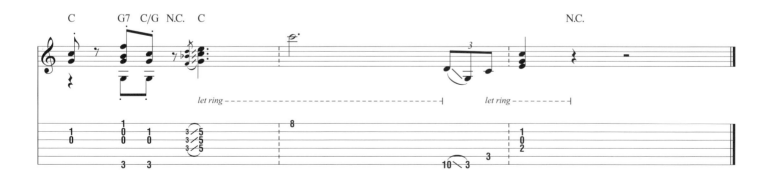

from *The Big Bill Broonzy Story*

Goin Down This Road Feelin Bad

Words and Music by William Lee Conley Broonzy

Tune down 1/4 step

Verse
Very fast ♩ = 184

1.I'm go-ing down _ this road, now, feel-ing bad, _____ ba - by. _ I'm

Gtr. 1 (acous.)

mf

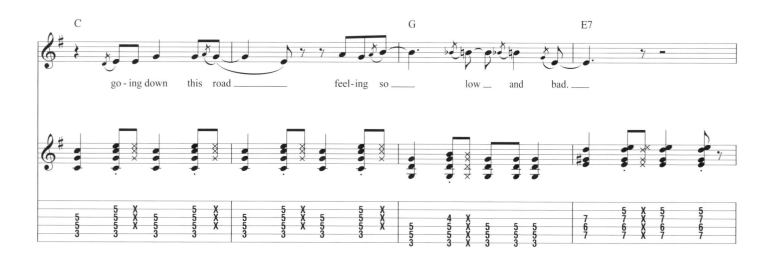

go-ing down this road _____ feel-ing so _____ low _ and bad. _____

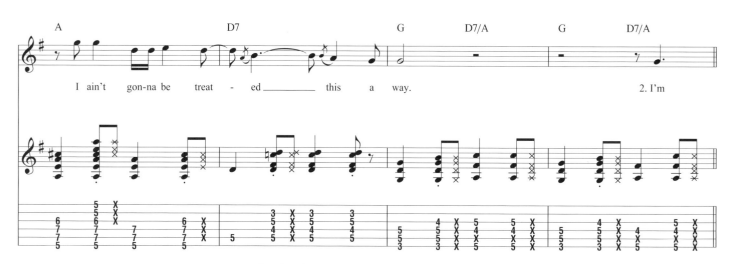

I ain't gon-na be treat - ed _____ this a way. 2. I'm

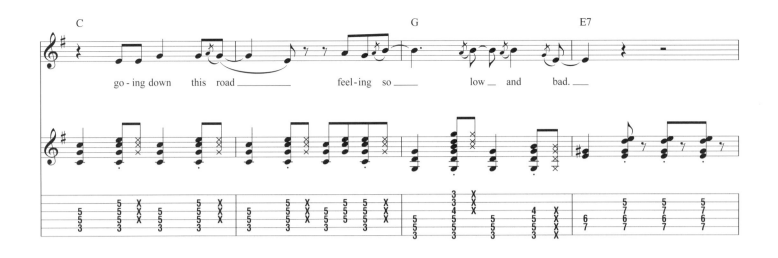

go-ing down this road _____ feel-ing so _____ low ____ and bad. ____

Free time

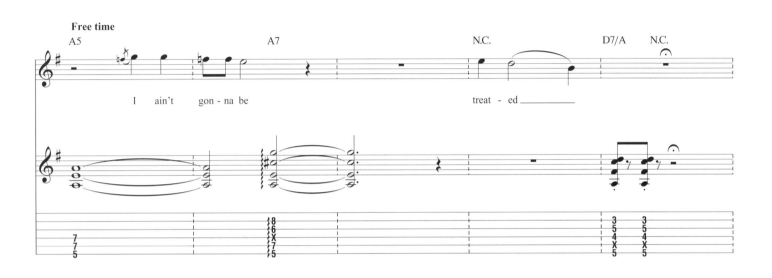

I ain't gon-na be treat-ed _____

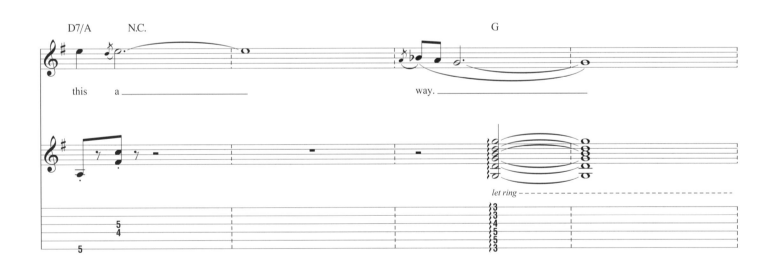

this a _____ way. _____

let ring - - - - - - - - - - - - - - - -

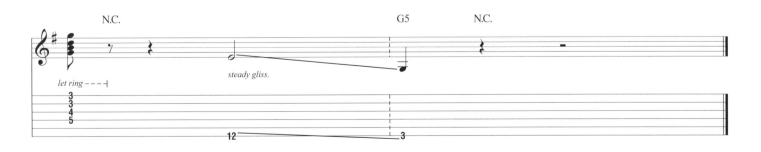

let ring - - -   *steady gliss.*

from *The Big Bill Broonzy Story*

Key to the Highway

Words and Music by William Lee Conley Broonzy and Chas. Segar

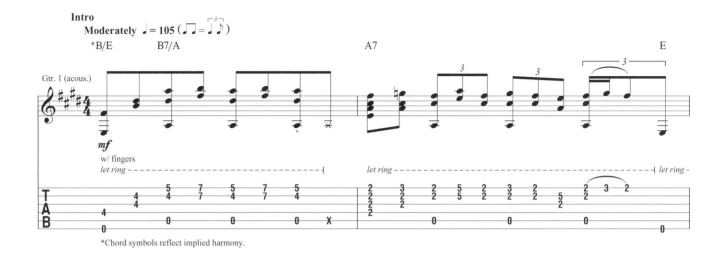

*Chord symbols reflect implied harmony.

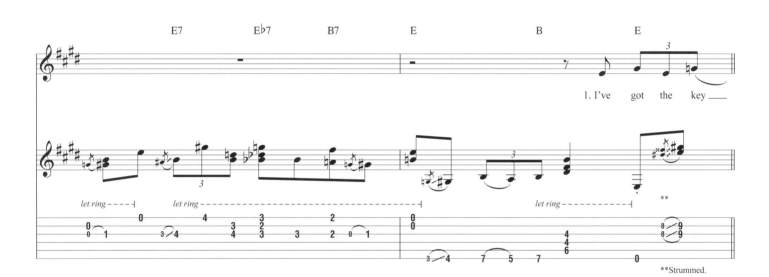

billed out   and   bound to go. ___   I'm gon-na leave, ___   leave   here   run-ning ___

be-cause walk-ing is   most ___ too   slow.   2. I'm   go - ing   down ___

*Strummed.

Verse

___   on the bor - der,   yeah, _____ ba -

Rhy. Fig. 1

**As before

Interlude

*Strummed.

Verse

Gtr. 1: w/ Rhy. Fig. 1

more kiss, ba - by,
peeps o - ver the moun - tain,

yeah, _____
yeah, _____ you know

____ just be - fore I go. ____
____ I'll be on my way. ____

'Cause when I leave you this time, _ now, ba - by,
I'm gon - na walk, ____ walk this old high - way,

I de - clare I won't be back ____ no more. ____
babe, un - til the break _ of day. ____

5. Now, when the moon ____
6. So long ____

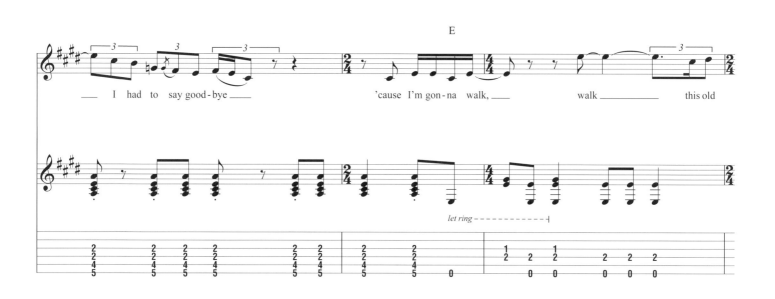

*Strummed.

from *Trouble in Mind*

Hey Hey

Words and Music by William Lee Conley Broonzy

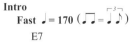

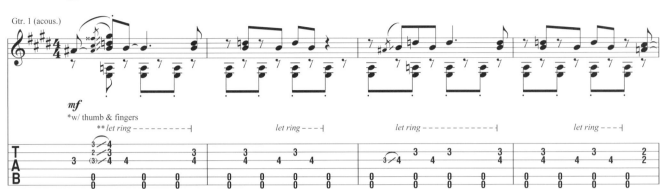

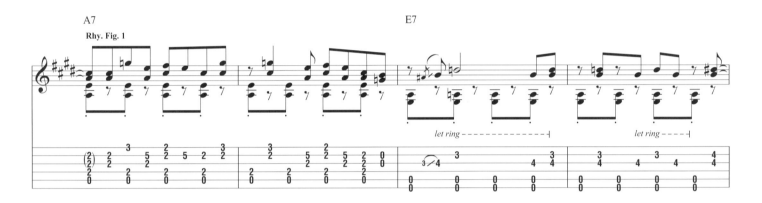

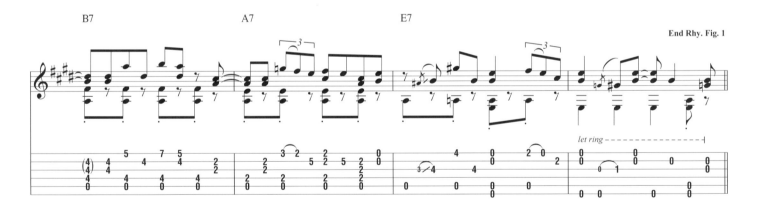

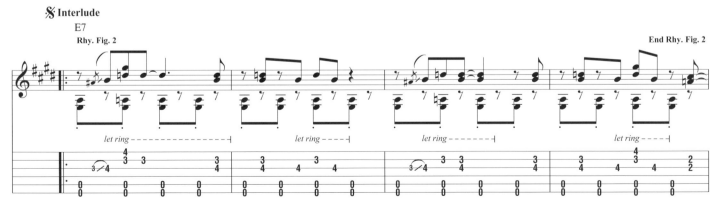

1st time, Gtr. 1: w/ Rhy. Fig. 1, simile
2nd & 3rd times, Gtr. 1: w/ Rhy. Fig. 1 (1st 7 meas., simile)

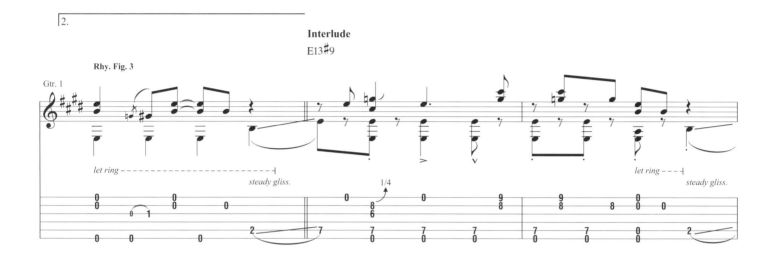

To Coda ⊕

2nd time, Gtr. 1: w/ Rhy. Fill 1, simile

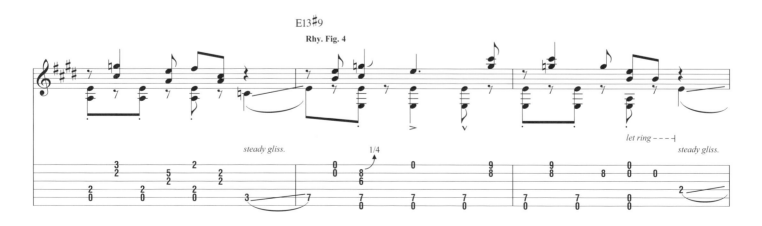

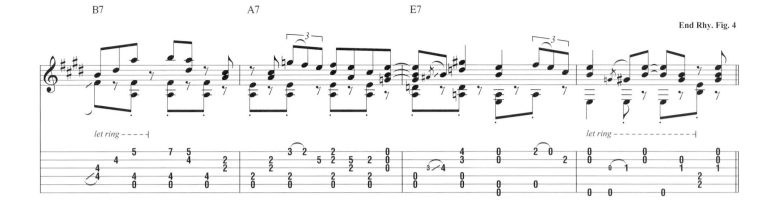

Chorus

Hey, hey. ____ Hey, hey, ba - by, hey. ____

Rhy. Fig. 5

Hey, hey. ____ Hey, hey, ba - by, hey. ____

Verse

Gtr. 1: w/ Rhy. Fig. 5, simile

1. Love you, babe, __ but I __ hate your __ dirt-y way. __

Love you, babe, __ but I __ hate your __ dirt-y way. __

Gtr. 1: w/ Rhy. Fig. 3

Ba-by, this time I'm __ go-ing a-way __ to stay. __

Interlude

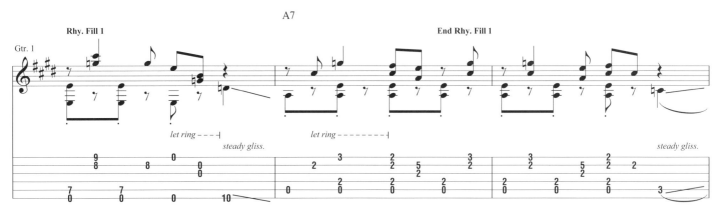

Gtr. 1: w/ Rhy. Fig. 4

E13#9   B7

D.S. al Coda
(take 2nd ending)

A7   E7

⊕ Coda

E13#9

Gtr. 1: w/ Rhy. Fig. 4 (last 4 meas.)

B7   A7   E7

Outro

Gtr. 1: w/ Rhy. Fig. 2, simile

E7

Gtr. 1: w/ Rhy. Fig. 1 (1st 6 meas., simile)

A7   E7

B7   A7

E7   N.C.

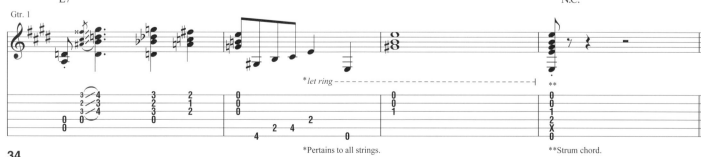

*Pertains to all strings.   **Strum chord.

See See Rider

Words and Music by Ma Rainey

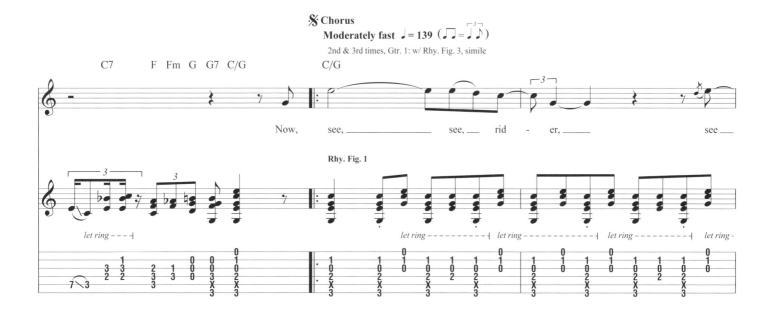

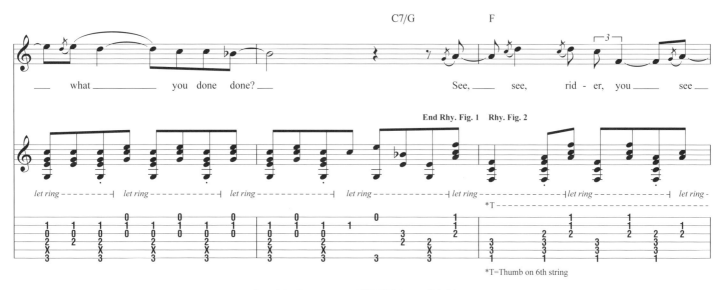

*T=Thumb on 6th string

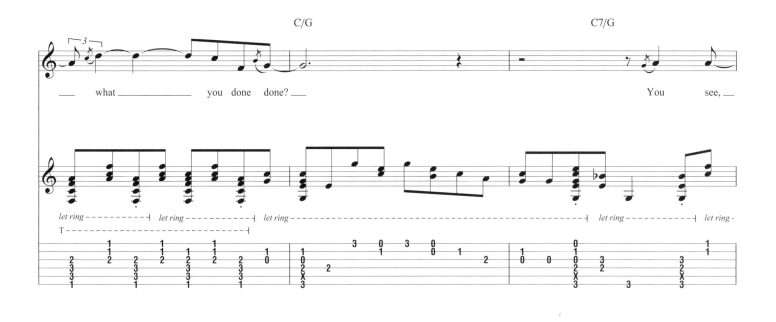

what _____ you done done? _____ You see, _____

_____ see, rid-er, you _____ see _____ what _____ you done done? _____ You have made _____

_____ me love _____ you and now _____ your man _____ done come. _____

1. My
2. I

Verse

2nd time, Gtr. 1: w/ Rhy. Fig. 1, simile

home _____ is on the wa - ter,   I don't like _____ no _____ land at all. _____   Home's
love _____ you, ba - by,   but I hate _____ your lit - tle dirt - y way. _____   Love

Gtr. 1: w/ Rhy. Fig. 2, simile

_____ on the wa - ter and I don't _ like _____ no _____ land _ at all. _____   My home's _
_____ you, ba - by, but I _____ hate _____ your dirt - y way. _____   You know I love _

_____ on the wa - ter and I don't _ like _____ no _____ land _ at all. _____   I'd ra -
_____ you, ba - by, but I _____ hate _____ your dirt - y way.   When I leave _

2nd time, D.S. al Coda

ther be dead _ than to stay _____ here and be _____ your dog. _____
_____ you this _ time, _ gal, I'm go - ing a - way _ to stay. _____

So, you

⊕ Coda

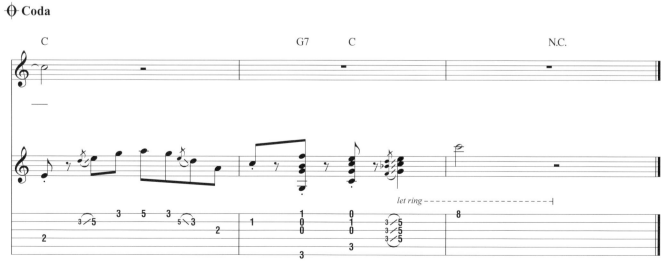

It Hurts Me Too

Words and Music by Mel London

Tune down 1/4 step

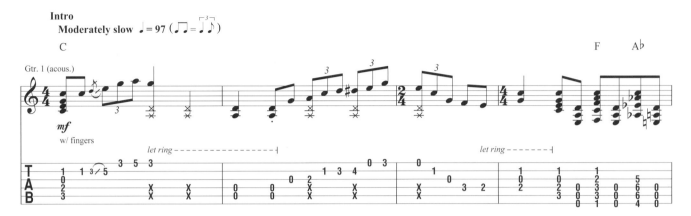

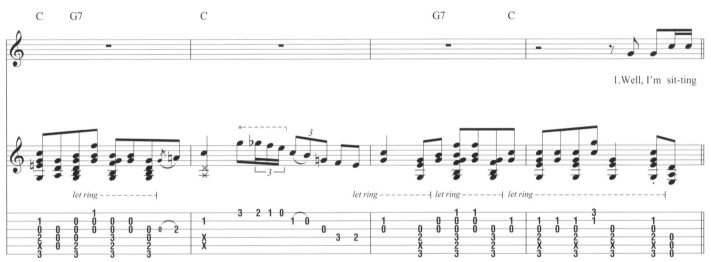

*Played as even eighth-notes.

Verse

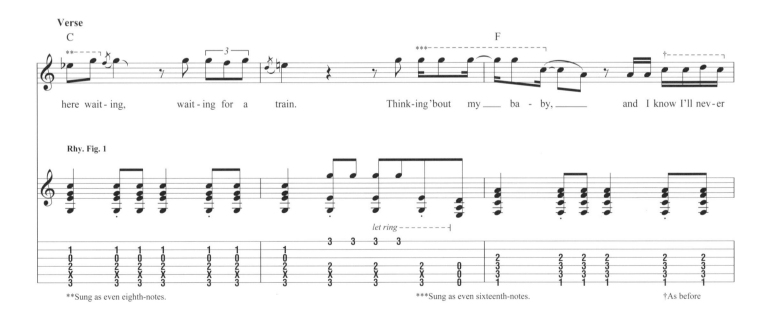

**Sung as even eighth-notes.   ***Sung as even sixteenth-notes.   †As before

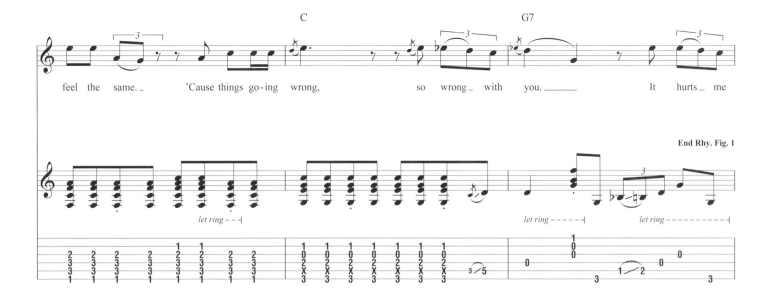

feel the same. ___ 'Cause things go-ing wrong, so wrong ___ with you. _____ It hurts ___ me

End Rhy. Fig. 1

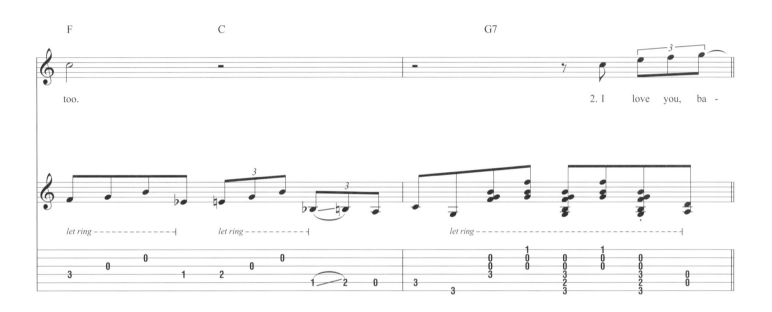

too. 2. I love you, ba -

Verse

Gtr. 1: w/ Rhy. Fig. 1, simile

- by, _____ no one else will do. You know I want you, ba - by, _____ and you know that it's

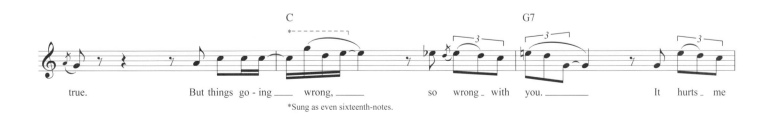

true. But things go - ing _____ wrong, _____ so wrong ___ with you. _____ It hurts ___ me

*Sung as even sixteenth-notes.

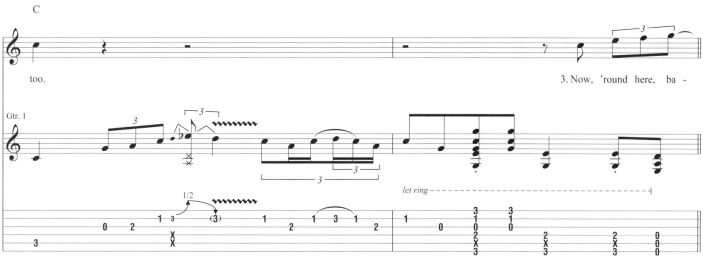

too.

3. Now, 'round here, ba -

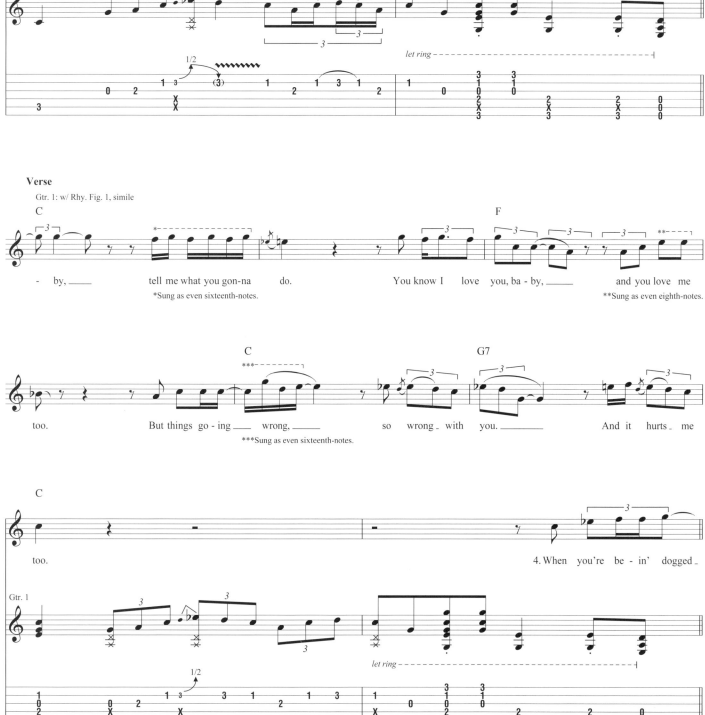

Verse

Gtr. 1: w/ Rhy. Fig. 1, simile

- by, ____ tell me what you gon-na do. You know I love you, ba - by, ____ and you love me

*Sung as even sixteenth-notes.

**Sung as even eighth-notes.

too. But things go - ing ____ wrong, ____ so wrong ____ with you. ____ And it hurts ____ me

***Sung as even sixteenth-notes.

too.

4. When you're be - in' dogged ____

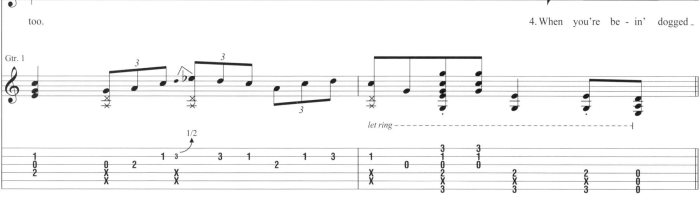

Verse

Gtr. 1: w/ Rhy. Fig. 1, simile

____ and pushed a - round. ____ I feel the same way, ba - by, ____ long as I'm in your ____

town.   'Cause things go-ing wrong,   so wrong with you.____   It hurts__ me

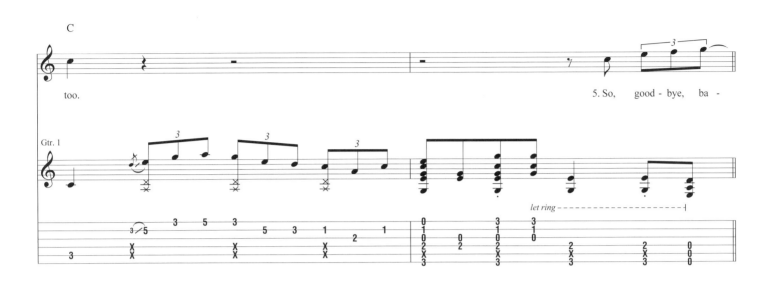

too.   5. So,   good-bye, ba -

Verse

Gtr. 1: w/ Rhy. Fig. 1 (1st 5 meas., simile)

- by, ____   I hate to go. ____   But I can tell the way you're act-ing   you can use____

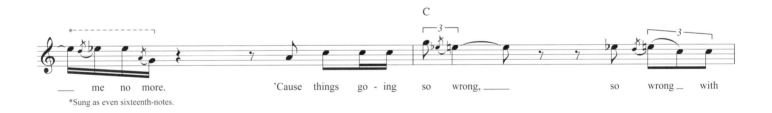

____ me no more.   'Cause things go-ing so wrong, ____   so wrong__ with

*Sung as even sixteenth-notes.

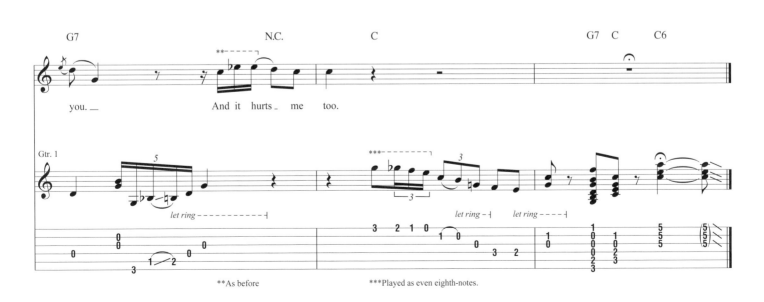

you. ____   And it hurts__ me too.

**As before   ***Played as even eighth-notes.

Lonesome Road Blues
By William Lee Conley Broonzy and John L. Hooker

Tune down 1/4 step

Intro
Slow ♩ = 70

*Pertains to strings 1-3 only throughout, except where indicated.

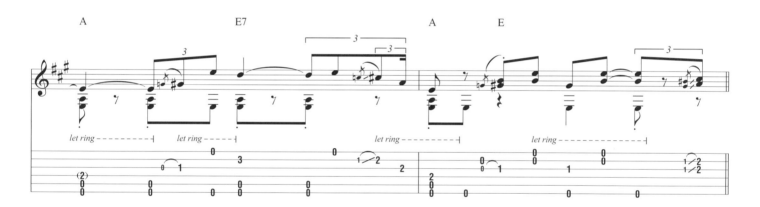

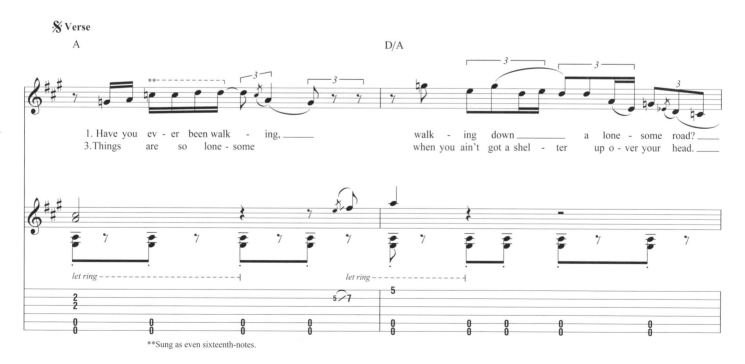

1. Have you ev - er been walk - ing, ____ walk - ing down ____ a lone - some road? ____
3. Things are so lone - some when you ain't got a shel - ter up o - ver your head. ____

Verse

A   D/A

**Sung as even sixteenth-notes.

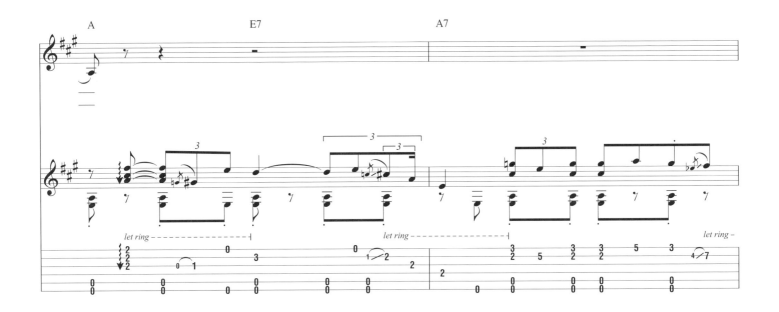

Have you ev - er been walk - ing, ___
Things look so lone - some ___

ba - by, walk-ing down ___ a lone - some road? ___
when you ain't got a shel - ter up o-ver your head. ___

Rhy. Fig. 1

Nah, ___
Yeah, ___

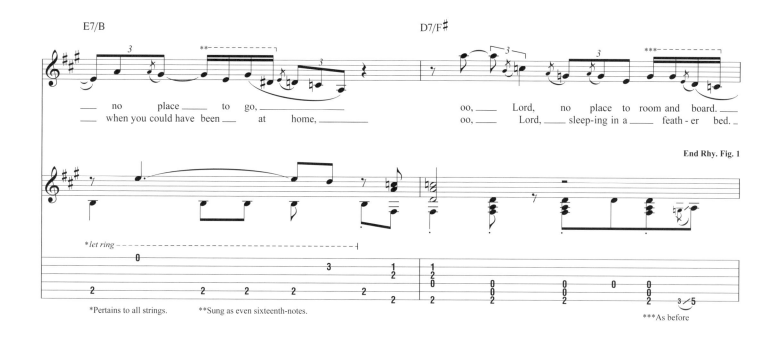

*Pertains to all strings.   **Sung as even sixteenth-notes.   ***As before

Verse

†Sung as even sixteenth-notes.

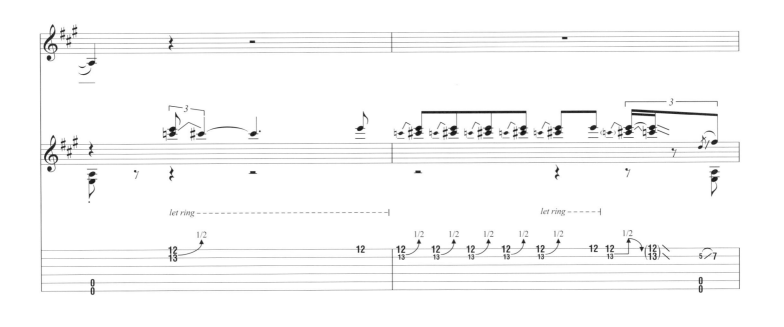

Gtr. 1: w/ Rhy. Fig. 1, simile

D7/A

Things look so ____ dark, ____ ba - by, down ____ that road a - head. ____

*Sung as even sixteenth-notes.

A   E7   A

Yeah, ____

E7/B   D7/F#

____ when you get to think-ing 'bout no place to live, _ no, ____ did-n't lis-ten to what your moth - er said. ____

**Sung as even sixteenth-notes.

D.S. al Coda

A   E7   A   E

Gtr. 1

Coda

Verse

A

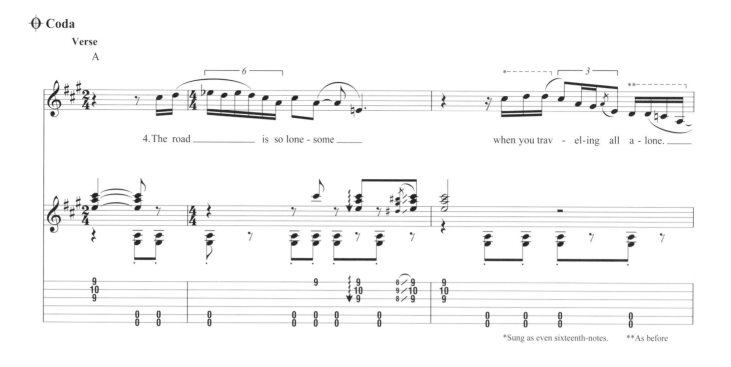

4. The road _____ is so lone - some _____ when you trav - el-ing all a - lone. _____

*Sung as even sixteenth-notes.   **As before

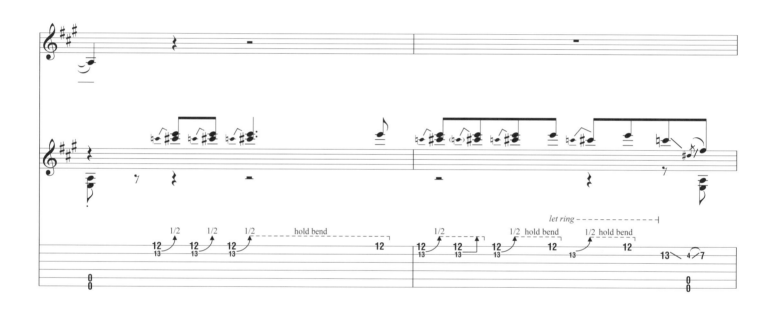

D/A

The roads _ are so lone - some _____ when you trav - el - ing _____ all a - lone. _____

***Sung as even sixteenth-notes.

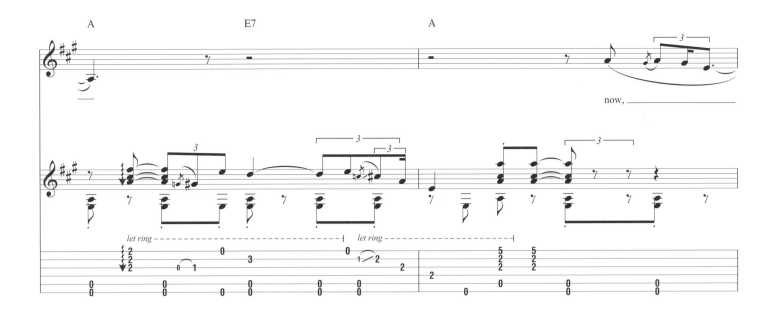

*Sung as even sixteenth-notes.

from *Just a Dream*

Long Tall Mama

Words and Music by William Lee Conley Broonzy

Tune down 1/4 step

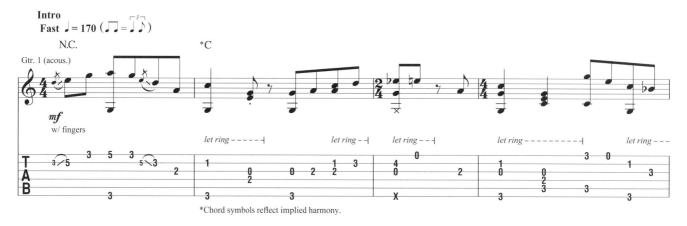

*Chord symbols reflect implied harmony.

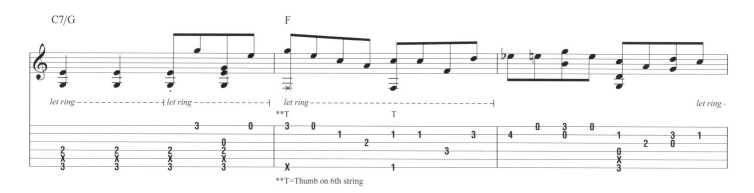

**T=Thumb on 6th string

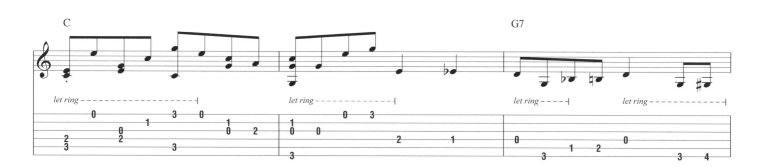

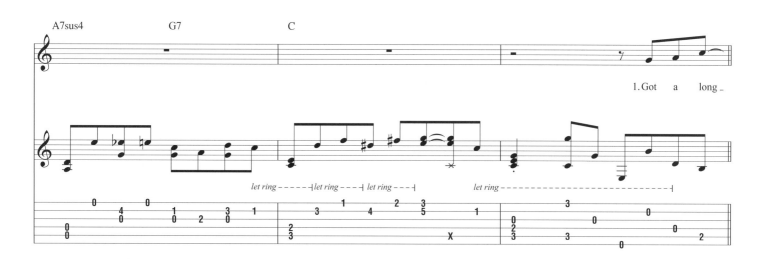

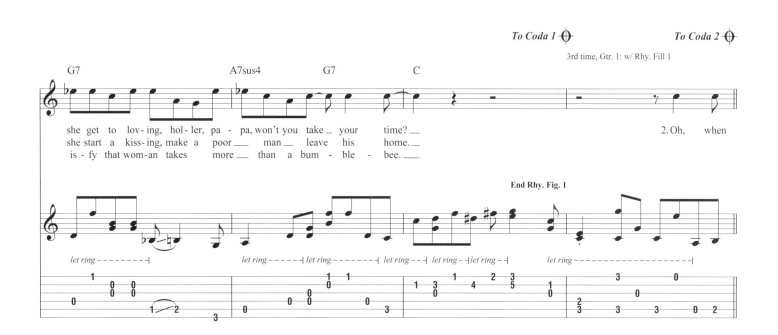

Verse

Gtr. 1: w/ Rhy. Fig. 1

she start a lov-ing, she sure ___ can ___ do her stuff. Oh, ___ when

she start a lov-ing, oh, she sure ___ can ___ do her stuff. And she squeez-

-ing so tight, ___ hol-ler, ma-ma, lord-y, that's ___ e - nough. ___

Interlude

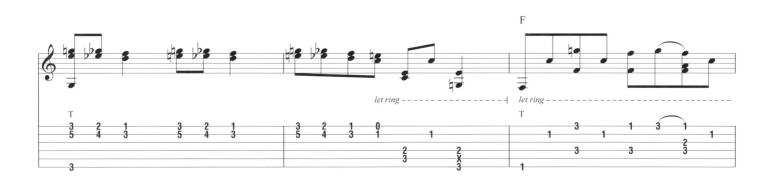

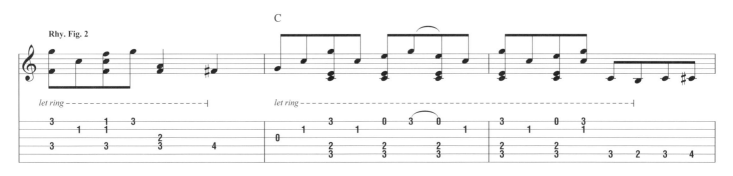

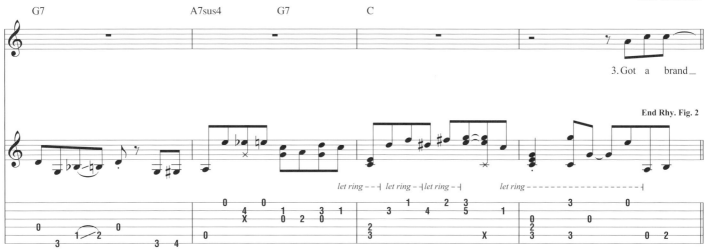

3. Got a brand__

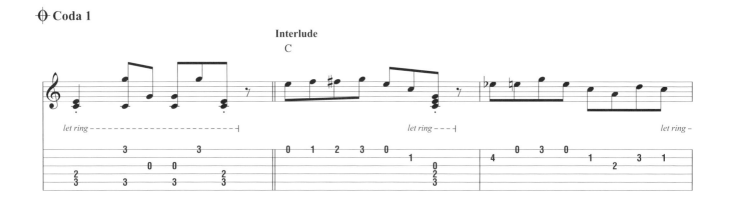

Coda 1

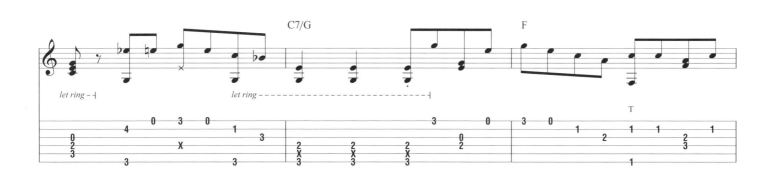

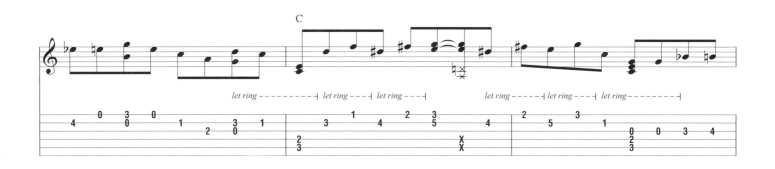

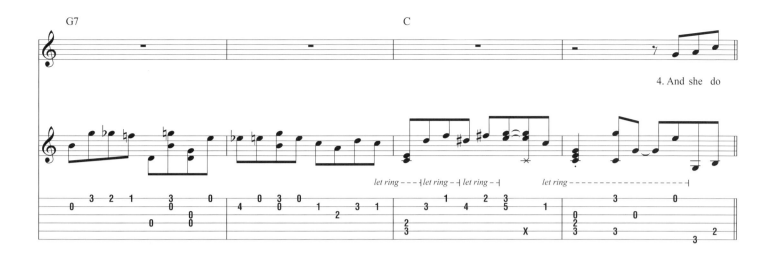

4. And she do

Verse

Gtr. 1: w/ Rhy. Fig. 1

a lit-tle of this, __ and, ma - ma, and she do a lit-tle of that.

Said she do

a lit-tle of this, __ ma - ma, Lord, __ and she do a lit-tle of that.

And when she

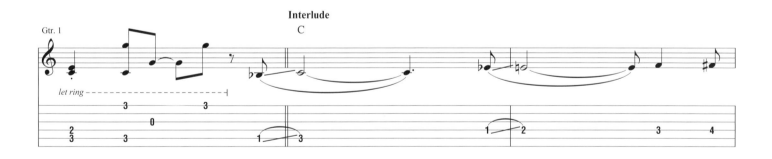

put on _____ full steam, make a freight __ train jump __ a track. __

Interlude

Gtr. 1

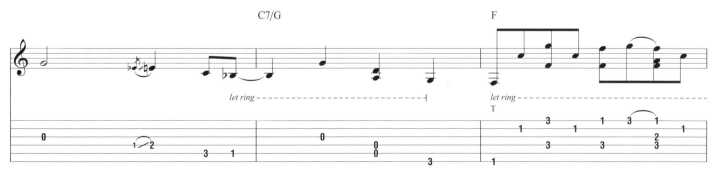

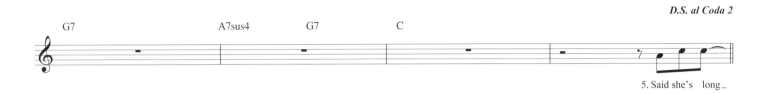

C

D.S. al Coda 2

G7　　　A7sus4　　G7　　　C

5. Said she's　long_

 Coda 2

Outro

C

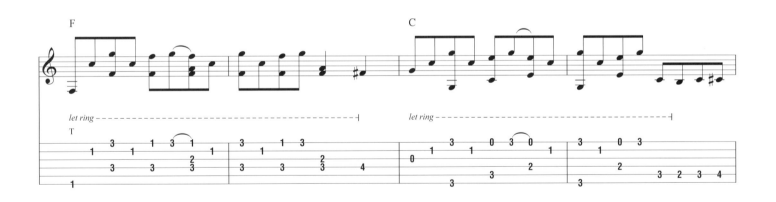

F　　　　　　　　　　　　　C

G7　　　A7sus4　　G7　　　C　　　　G7　　C

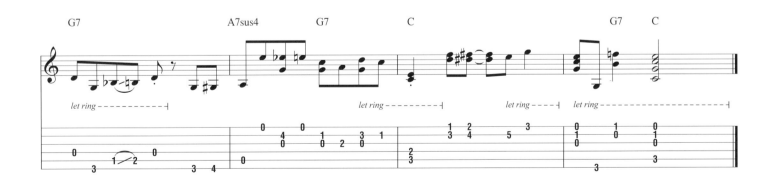

Southbound Train

Words and Music by William Lee Conley Broonzy

*Chord symbols reflect implied harmony.

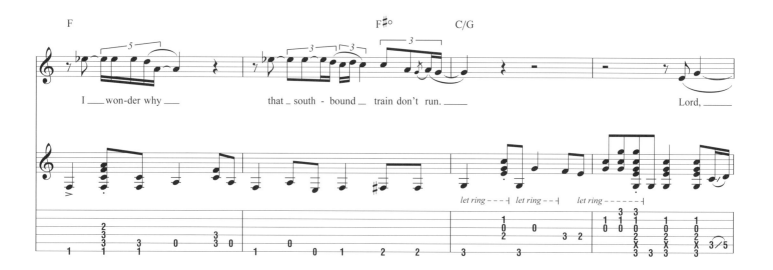

**Sung as even sixteenth-notes.

Verse

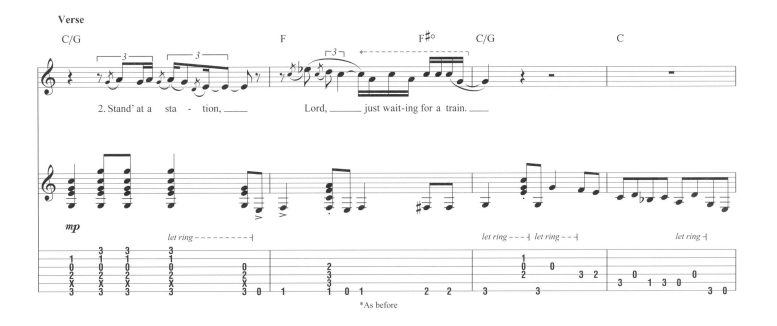

2. Stand' at a sta - tion, _____ Lord, _____ just wait-ing for a train. _____

*As before

I was stand' at a sta-tion, Lord, _____ just wait-ing for a train. _____ Lord, _____

**As before

_____ deep down in my poor heart, Lord, there lied _ an ach-ing pain. _____

***Sung as even eighth-notes.　　　　　†Sung as even sixteenth-notes.

Verse

3. Mis-ter con-duc-tor man, _ please _____ let me ride _ your train. _

*Sung as even sixteenth-notes.

Mis-ter con-duc-tor man, _ please _____ let me ride _ your train. _____ Lord, _____

**As before   ***As before

_____ I'm in trou-ble, _ and I'm _____ a mis-er-a-ble man. _____

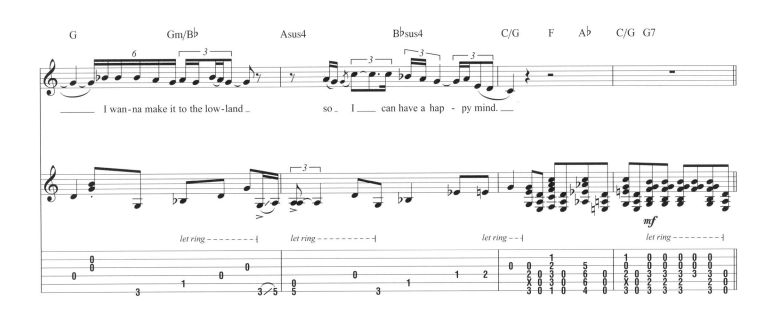

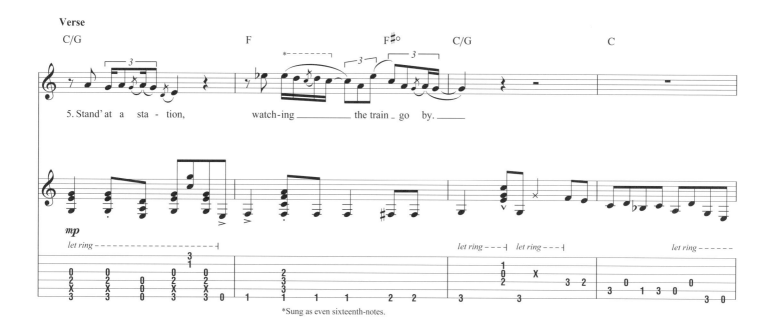

*Sung as even sixteenth-notes.

**As before

Trouble in Mind

Words and Music by Richard M. Jones

Tune down 1/4 step

*Chord symbols reflect implied harmony.

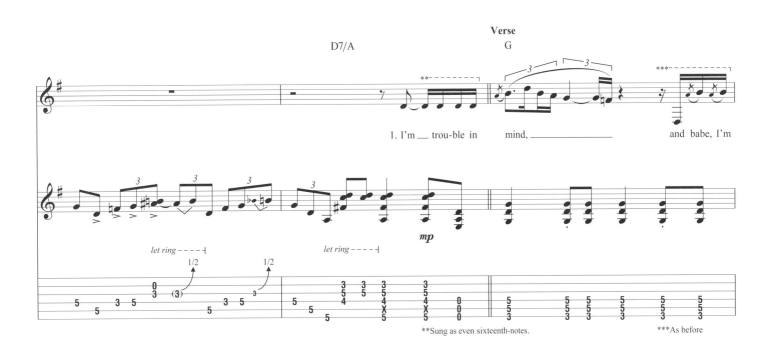

**Sung as even sixteenth-notes. ***As before

†As before

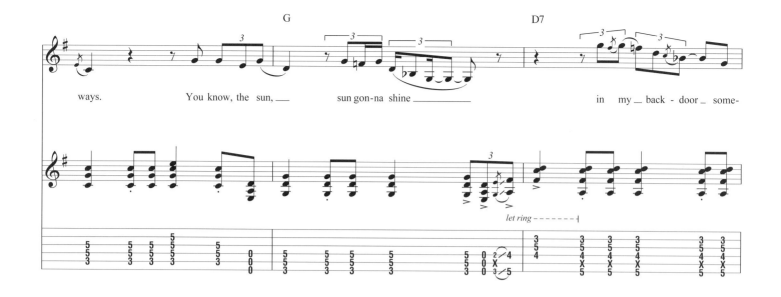

ways.   You know, the sun, ___   sun gon-na shine ___   in my ___ back-door ___ some-

day.   2. I'm go-ing down, ___

Verse

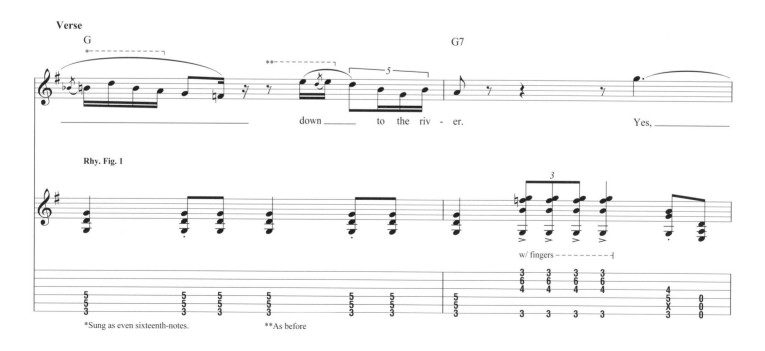

down ___   to the riv- er.   Yes, _____

Rhy. Fig. 1

w/ fingers

*Sung as even sixteenth-notes.   **As before

I'm gon - na take, _____ take my lit - tle rock - ing chair.

*As before

Now, if the blues, ___ blues o - ver - take me _____ I'm gon - na rock _ on a - way _ from here. _

End Rhy. Fig. 1

**As before

3.'Cause I'm trou - ble in

Verse

Gtr. 1: w/ Rhy. Fig. 1

mind, _____ and, babe, I'm so blue. Yes, _____

but I won't,   won't be blue al - ways.

*Sung as even sixteenth-notes.

You know, the sun,   sun gon-na shine   in my   back - door some -

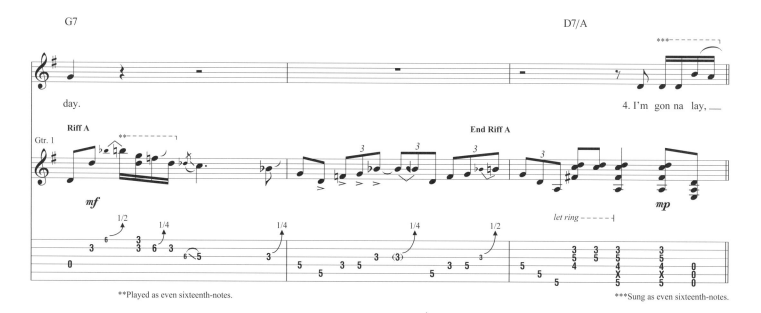

day.

4. I'm gon na lay,

**Played as even sixteenth-notes.

***Sung as even sixteenth-notes.

Verse

Gtr. 1: w/ Rhy. Fig. 1, simile

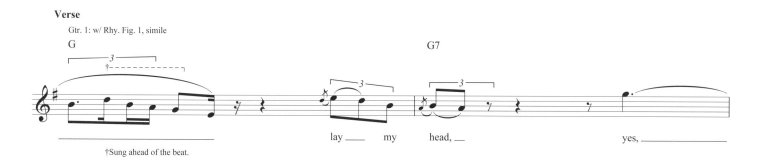

lay   my   head,   yes,

†Sung ahead of the beat.

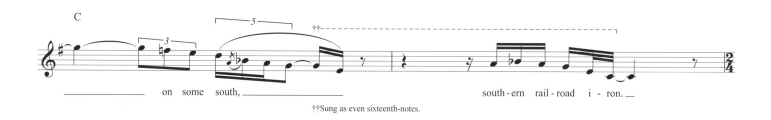

on some south,   south - ern rail - road i - ron.

††Sung as even sixteenth-notes.

I'm gon-na let that Two,   Two - Nine - teen, ba - by,   pac - i - fy my mind.

†††As before

*Played as even sixteenth-notes.

Verse

Gtr. 1: w/ Rhy. Fig. 1

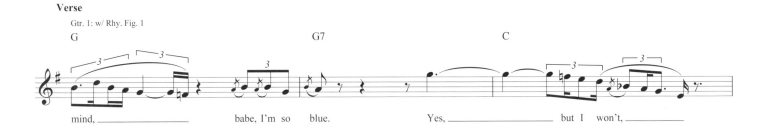

mind,_____ babe, I'm so blue. Yes, _____ but I won't, _____

won't be blue al-ways. You know, the sun, _____ sun gon-na shine _____

**Sung as even sixteenth-notes.

Gtr. 1: w/ Riff A

in my __ back-door some - day.

Free time

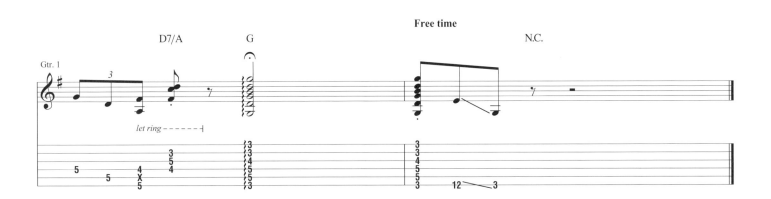

Willie Mae

Words and Music by William Lee Conley Broonzy

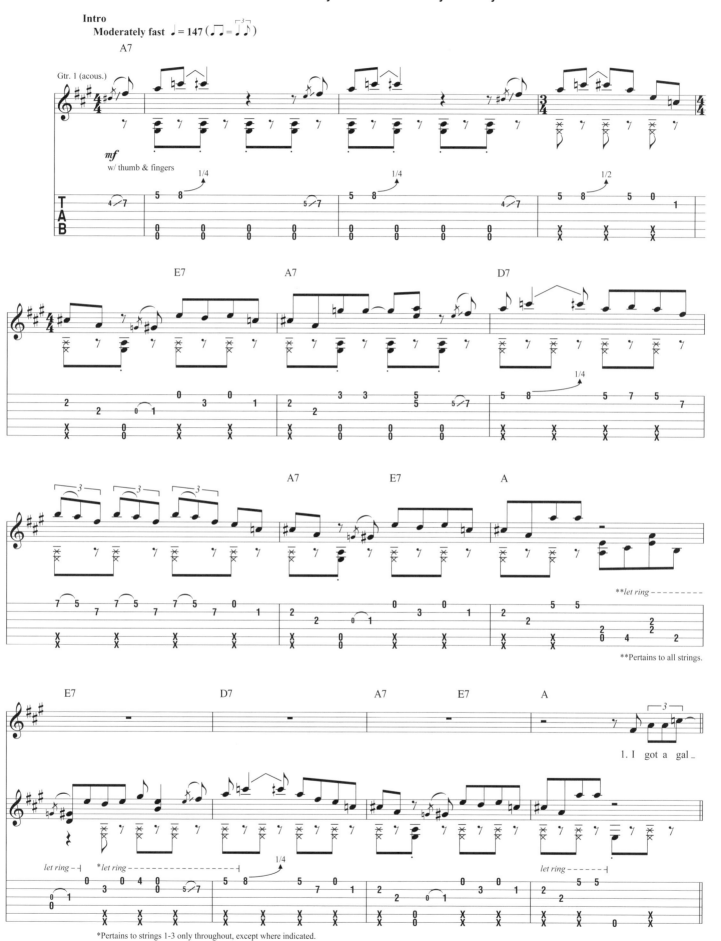

Intro
Moderately fast ♩ = 147

*Pertains to strings 1-3 only throughout, except where indicated.

**Pertains to all strings.

Verse

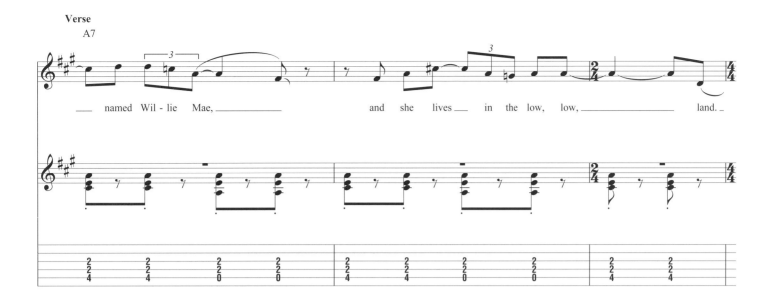

named Wil-lie Mae, _____ and she lives _____ in the low, low, _____ land. _____

I got a gal _____ named Wil lie Mae _____ and she lives _____

_____ in the low, low, _____ land. _____ Lord, _____ the way I _____ got _____

*Pertains to all strings.

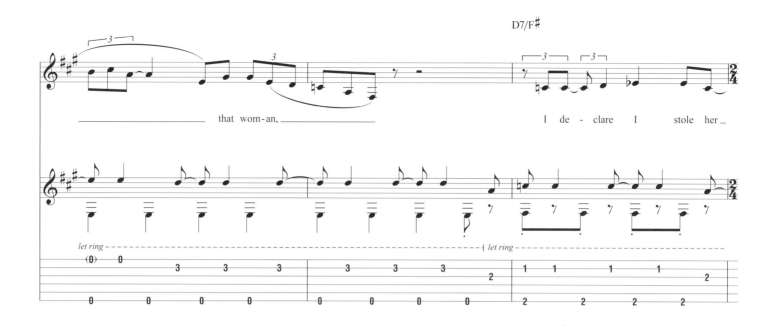

that wom-an, I de-clare I stole her

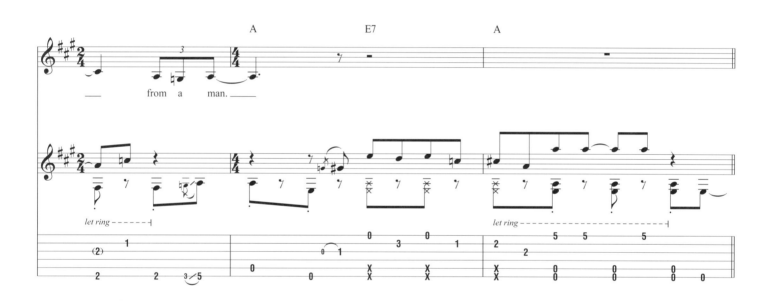

from a man.

Verse

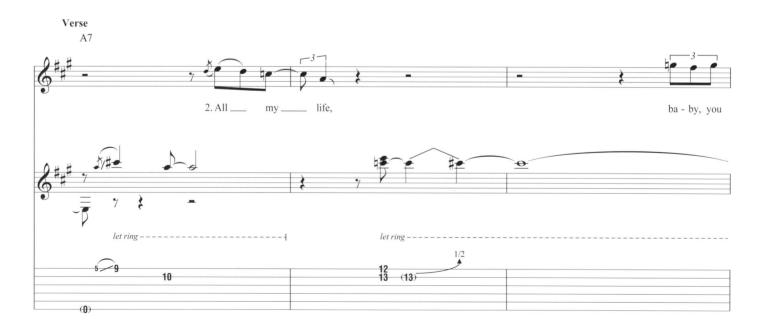

2. All my life, ba-by, you

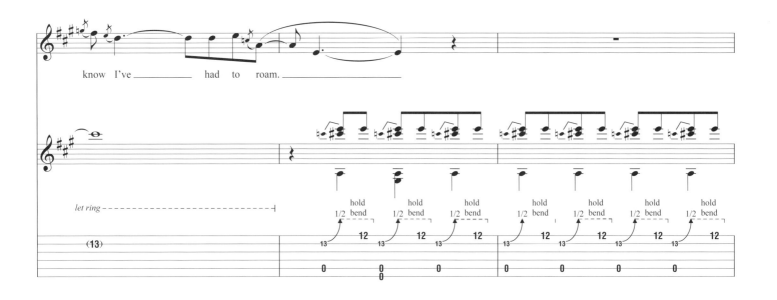

know I've _____ had to roam. _____

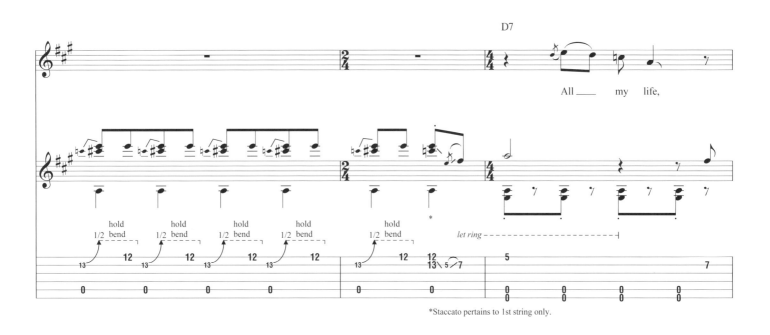

D7

All _____ my life,

*Staccato pertains to 1st string only.

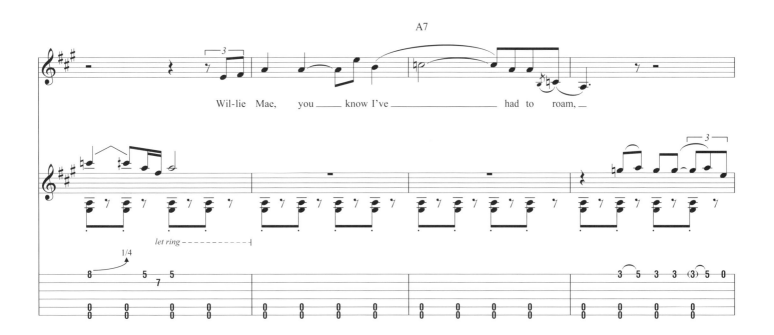

A7

Wil-lie Mae, you _____ know I've _____ had to roam, __

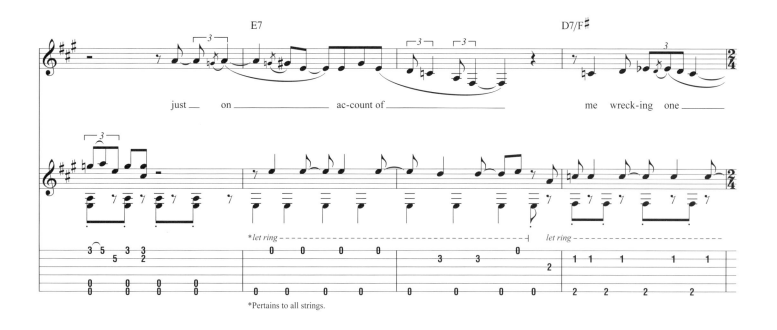

just on ac-count of me wreck-ing one

*let ring
*Pertains to all strings.

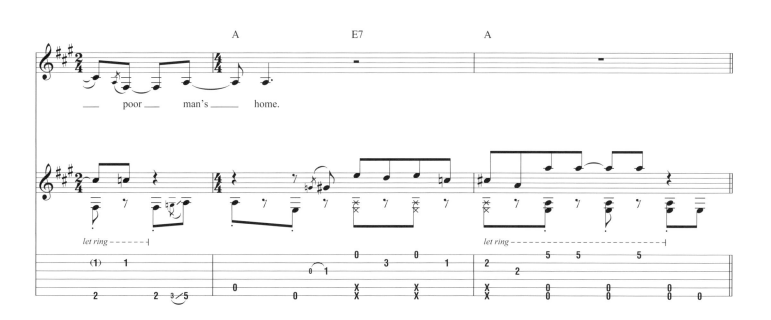

poor man's home.

let ring

Chorus
A7

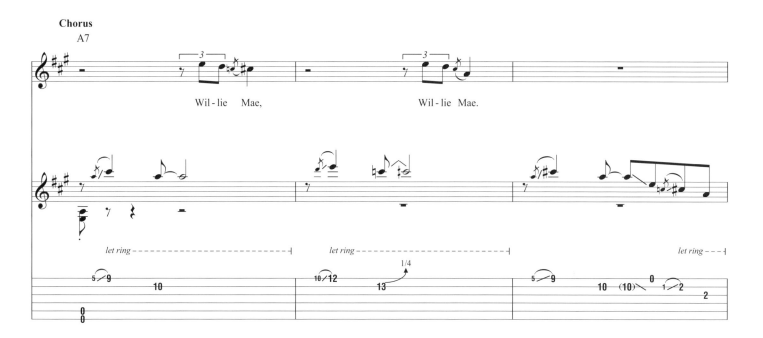

Wil-lie Mae, Wil-lie Mae.

let ring

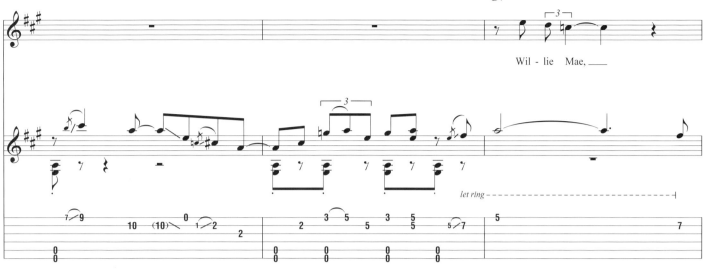

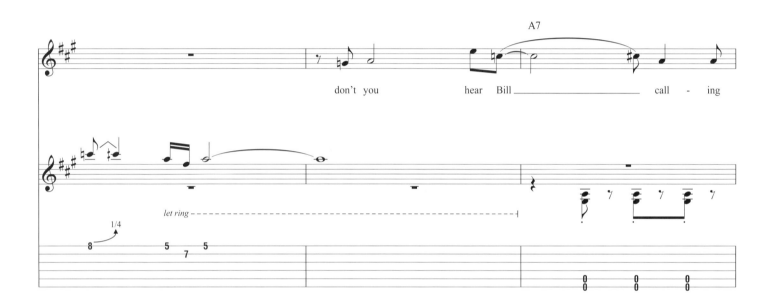

Wil - lie Mae, ___

don't you ___ hear Bill ___ call - ing

you? ___

Lord, ___ if I don't

get ___

*Pertains to all strings.

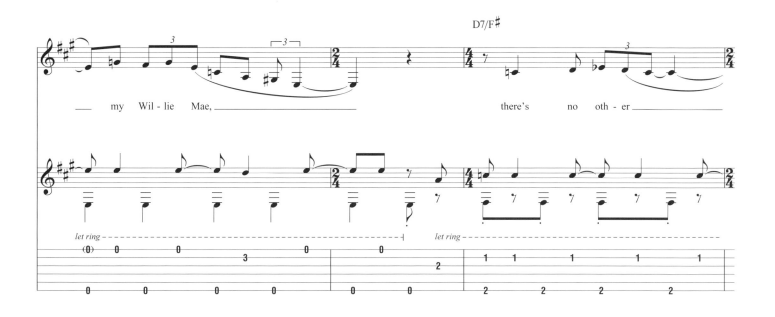

_ my Wil - lie Mae, _____ there's no oth - er _____

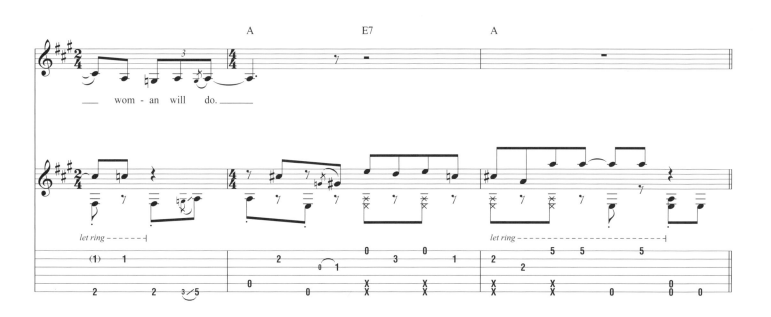

_ wom - an will do. _____

Verse

3. When I get to think-ing 'bout Wil-lie Mae, _____ cold chill creeps up and down _ my spine. _

*steady gliss.

*Pertains to all strings.

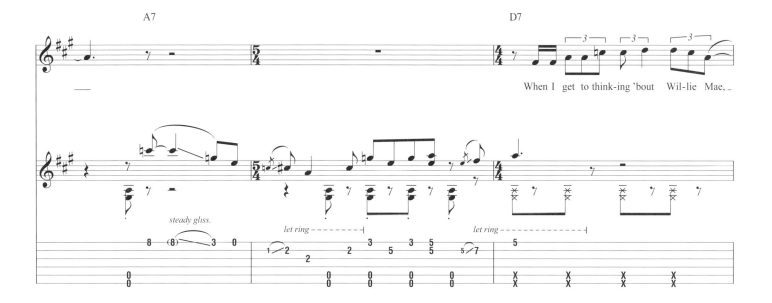

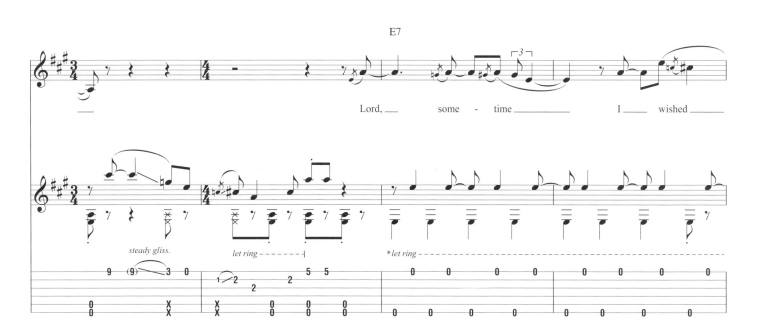

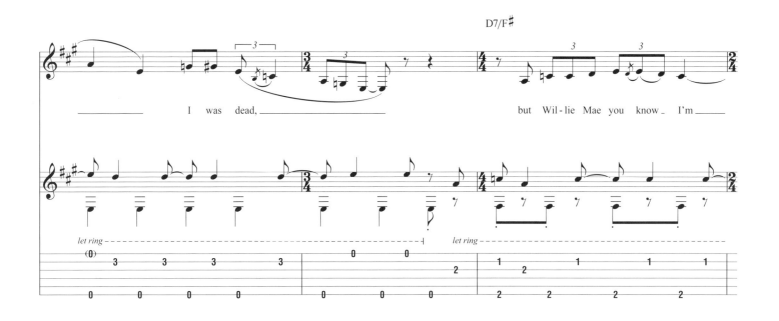

I was dead, _____ but Wil-lie Mae you know_ I'm _____

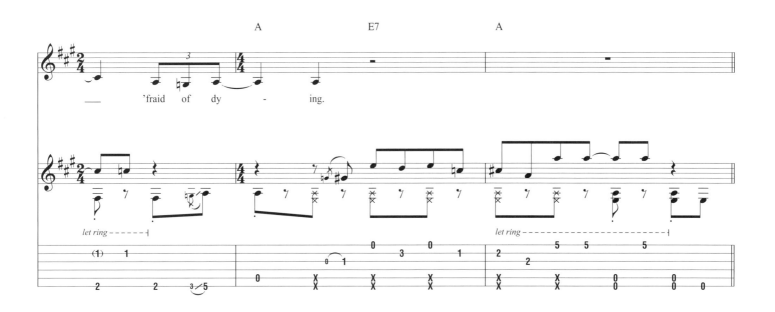

_____ 'fraid of dy - ing.

Verse

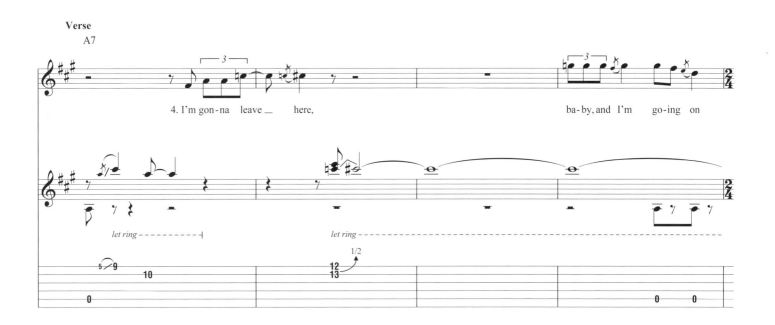

4. I'm gon-na leave _ here, ba-by, and I'm go-ing on

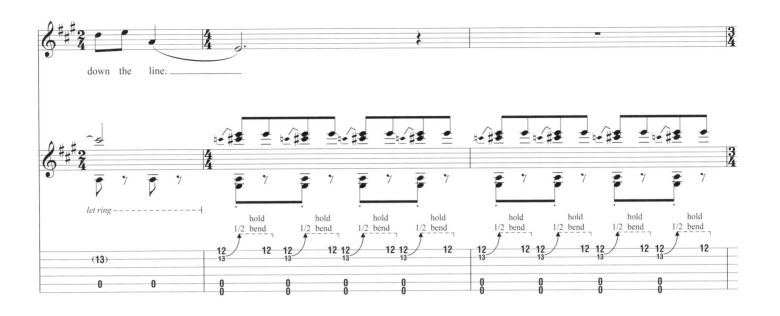

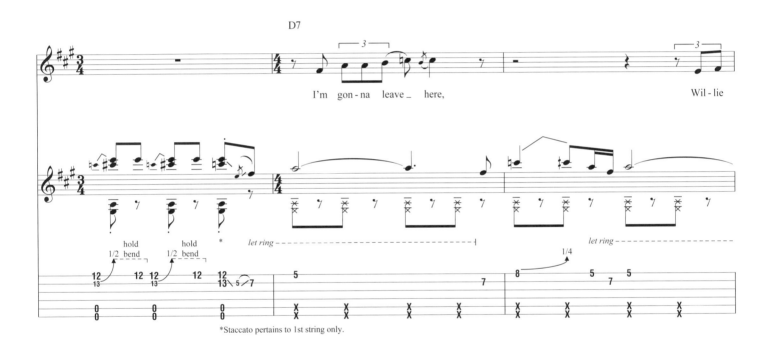

*Staccato pertains to 1st string only.

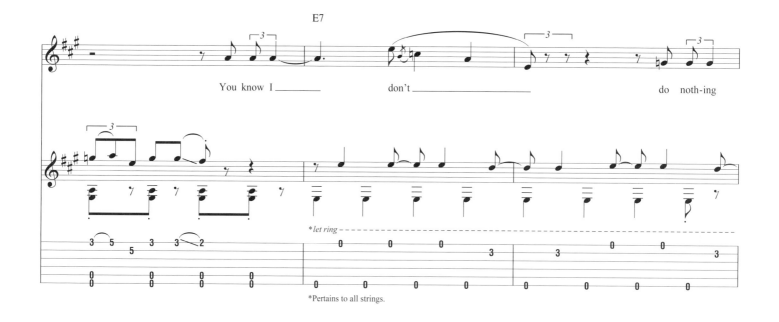

You know I _____ don't _____ do noth-ing

*Pertains to all strings.

here, _____ Wil - lie Mae, _____ but grieve and cry. _____

You know I _____

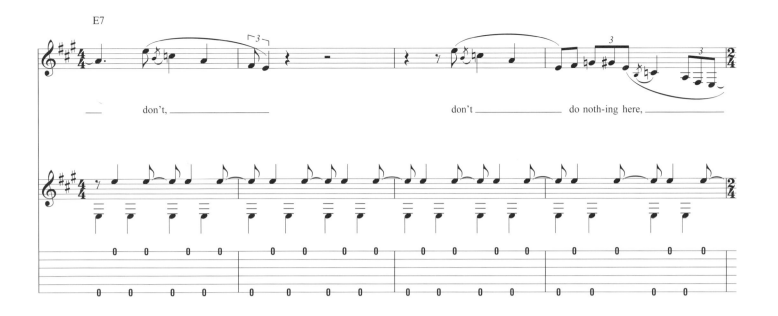

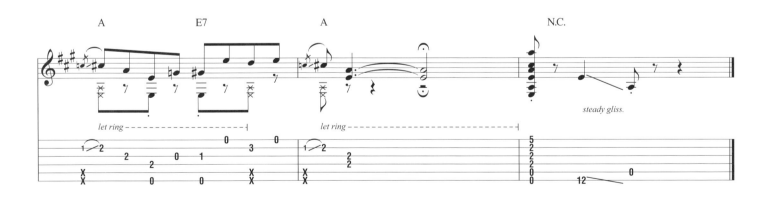

from *The Big Bill Broonzy Story*

Worried Life Blues

Words and Music by Maceo Merriweather

Tune down 1 step:
(low to high) D-G-C-F-A-D

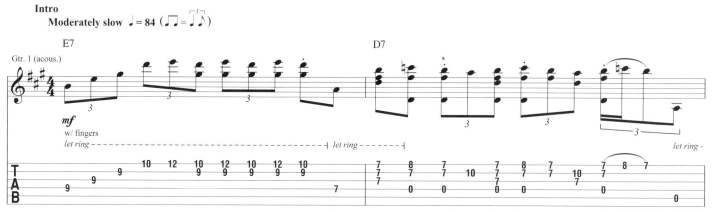

*Staccato marks pertain to 4th string only, this meas.

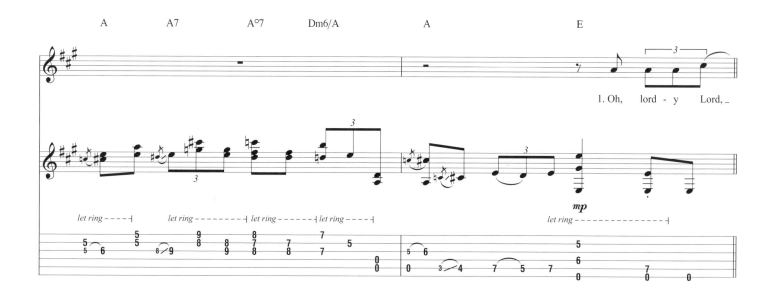

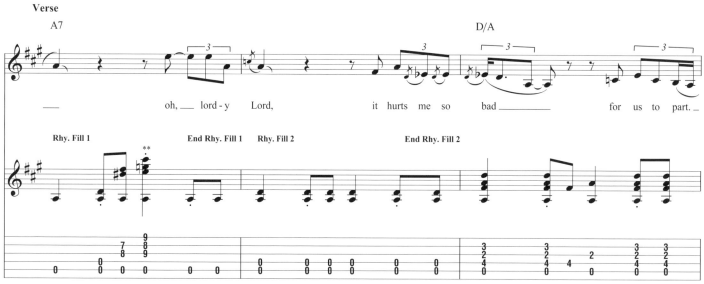

**Staccato mark pertains to 5th string only.

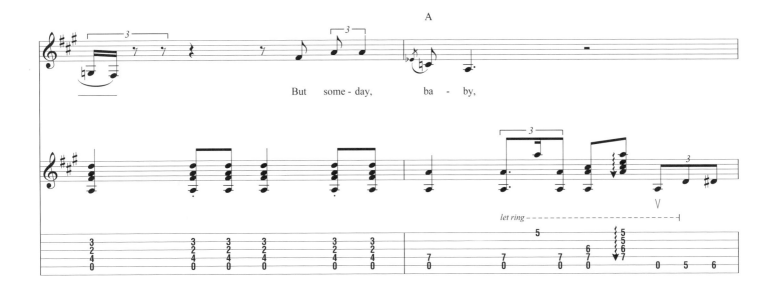

But some-day, ba - by,

you ain't gon-na wor - - ry my life an-y-more. _____

Verse

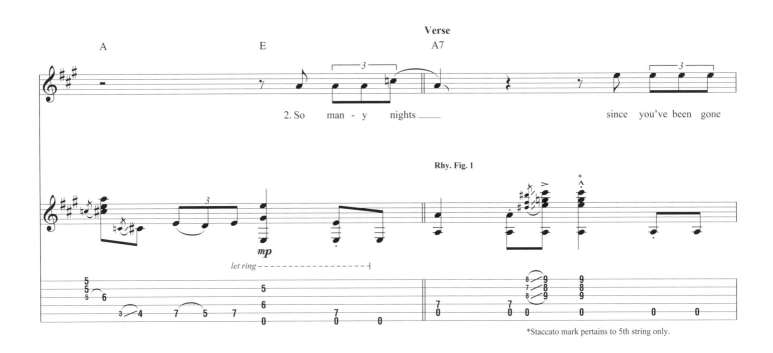

2. So man - y nights _____ since you've been gone

Rhy. Fig. 1

*Staccato mark pertains to 5th string only.

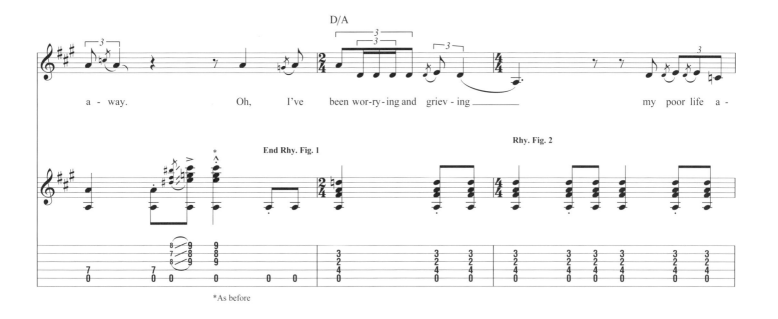

a - way.   Oh,   I've   been wor-ry-ing and griev - ing _____   my poor life a -

*As before

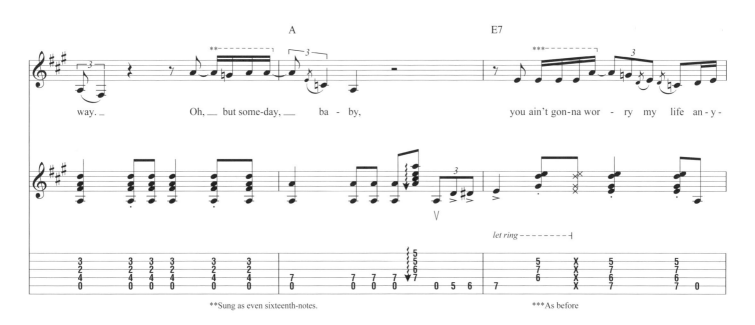

way. _   Oh, _ but some-day, _   ba - by,   you ain't gon-na wor - ry   my   life   an-y-

**Sung as even sixteenth-notes.   ***As before

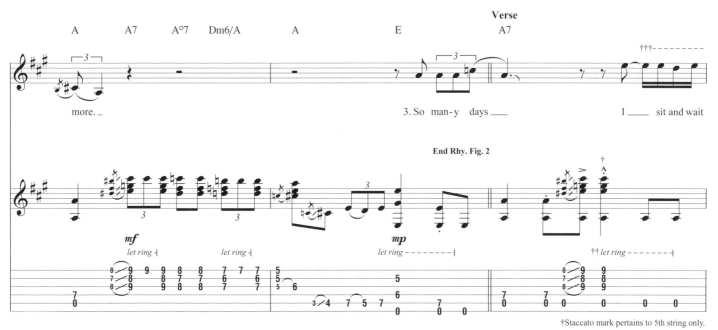

more. _   3. So man-y days _   I _ sit and wait

†Staccato mark pertains to 5th string only.
††Pertains to top 3 strings only.
†††Sung as even sixteenth-notes.

D/A

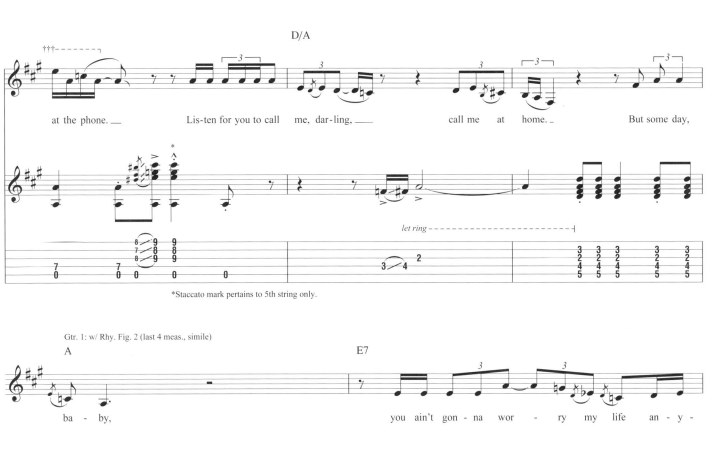

at the phone. ___   Lis-ten for you to call   me, dar-ling, ___   call me   at   home. ___   But some day,

*Staccato mark pertains to 5th string only.

Gtr. 1: w/ Rhy. Fig. 2 (last 4 meas., simile)

A   E7

ba - by,   you ain't gon - na wor - ry my life an - y -

A   A7   A°7   Dm6/A   A   E

more. ___   4. So,   you's   on   my

Verse

Gtr. 1: w/ Rhy. Fill 2   Gtr. 1: w/ Rhy. Fill 1

A7

mind _____   ev - 'ry   place   I   go.   That's al -

Gtr. 1: w/ Rhy. Fig. 2, simile

D/A

right, ba - by, _____   no - bod - y   in   this whole world know. ___   But   some - day,

A   E7

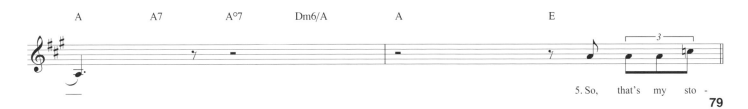

ba - by,   you ain't gon - na wor - ry poor Bill an - y - more. ___

A   A7   A°7   Dm6/A   A   E

___   5. So,   that's   my   sto -

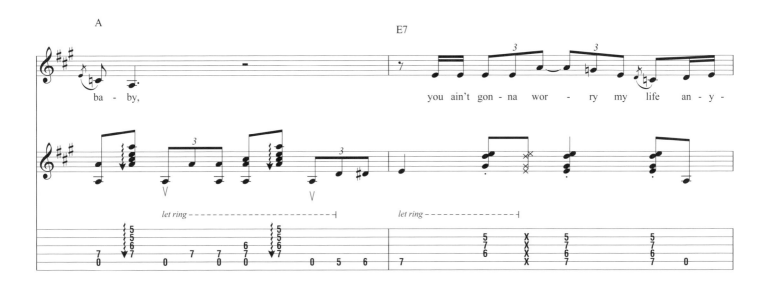